The Gentle People:

Personal Reflections
of Amish Life

by
Joe Wittmer, Ph.D.

**With Contributions From
Amish Children and Adults**

Dedication

This book is dedicated to the memory of my Amish father, William Wittmer, and to my two-year-old granddaughter, Raechel Diane Thompson. May she grow to appreciate her heritage.

Library of Congress Catalog Card No. 90-071047

ISBN 0-932796-32-X

Printing (Last Digit)

10 9 8 7 6 5 4 3 2 1

Publisher—

Box 21311
Minneapolis, MN 55421-0311

Production editor—Don L. Sorenson

Graphic design—Earl Sorenson

References and Acknowledgments

A very special thanks to the publishers of: *Young Companion* (published monthly); *Family Life* (published eleven times a year): and *Blackboard Bulletin* (published ten times annually). All are published by Pathway Publishers, Aylmer, Ontario N5H 2R3.

Every effort has been made to give proper acknowledgment to all those who have contributed to this book. Any omissions or errors are regretted and, upon notification, will be corrected in subsequent editions.

Table of Contents

The Author—Age 10

This photo of the author was found some time ago in the effects of a late aunt. I well remember posing for the taboo camera at about the age of ten. The cameraman was a non-Amish "driver" who had been employed to "carry" my aunt and her family from a distant Amish settlement to my sister's wedding. This is the only available photograph of me from that time in my life.

The Author

Dr. Joe Wittmer is a Professor of Counseling at the University of Florida, Gainesville. He was born and raised Old Order Amish and remained a participant for the first sixteen years of his life. He has written numerous magazine and journal articles regarding the Amish and is Vice-Chair of the National Committee for Amish Religious Freedom. Dr. Wittmer has also authored or co-authored six books in the area of counseling and teaching.

The Illustrator

Mrs. Sue Wittmer, M.A., is a Counselor at Santa Fe Community College, Gainesville, Florida.

More About the Author/Editor: Growing Up Amish

I am often asked what it is like to be an Amishman. Most Americans know them only by newspaper reports as a simple, virtuous people, who live on farms and use no electricity, automobiles, trucks, tractors, radios, television or other such "necessities" of modern life. Their broad-brimmed black hats, black buggies and past tussles with educational authorities all have further stereotyped the Amish as anachronisms in this space age. Their values, we are told, are of the past. Better than most people, I know what the Amish really are like, for I was born and reared in the Old Order Amish faith.

Religion on our Indiana farm was a seven-day-a-week affair. The way we dressed, the way we farmed, the way we talked—our whole lifestyle—was a daily reminder of our religion, as it is for all of America's Amish.

The fourth of six children, I learned the Amish way by a gradual process of kindly indoctrination. At five I was given a corner of the garden to plant and care for as my own and a small pig and calf to raise. Amishmen are either farmers or are in related occupations such as blacksmithing and buggy-making. My father had no doubt that I would someday be a God-fearing farmer like himself, and my stepmother often added in her German dialect, "and a nice black beard like your father's you will have yet."

Because Amish parochial schools were not yet in existence, I entered the strange world of public school at eight. My parents deliberately planned this late entry into school so that I would be sixteen, the minimum age for quitting, in the eighth grade. High school, to the Amish, is a "contaminating" influence that challenges the Biblical admonition to be a "peculiar people." No Old Order Amish children are permitted more than eight years of formal education. The Amish also resist education below the eighth grade if it originates in modern consolidated schools. America was at war with Germany when I entered the first grade. Without radios and newspapers or relatives fighting (all Amish are conscientious objectors), I had little opportunity at home to keep up with the progress of the war. School was another matter.

Boys played war games and talked constantly about the war and the branch of service they someday would join. Often I was asked where I would serve. I knew that as a conscientious objector I would never go to war.

I often wished that I could help the non-Amish children gather sacks of milkweed pods, used to make parachutes for American flyers. However, I was taught that to engage in activities that would further the war effort was sinful. Because I did not participate, I was often the object of derision.

The ordeal of Amish students reached its cruel peak during the daily pledge to the flag, which for religious reasons, our parents taught us not to salute or pledge allegiance to. The jibes of students and the disappointed looks of the teacher as we remained seated cut me deeply. How could I explain that the Amish believe in praying for all governments, which, they hold, are ordained by God? How could I explain that hate is not in the Amish vocabulary? Explain it, moreover, in a German accent, for German was the first language of all Amish youth because the church required it to be spoken at home.

In retrospect, I can understand all too well the feelings of the non-Amish students. I can understand also why the Amish have established their own schools. What was at stake was not only the feelings of Amish youth, but a way of life.

Few non-Amish understand the pressures on a nonconformist in the public school system. Many activities are strictly off limits to the Amish youth; not only dancing and other "worldly entertainments," but also class pictures and educational movies. When such activities were scheduled, we Amish children were herded into another room to the chiding and laughter of our classmates.

The pressure was always on us to conform to the majority way of life. My non-Amish schoolmates were taught that, in America, good guys wear white hats, not broad-brimmed black ones. Teachers made it plain that everyone should yearn for a college education—forbidden by our religion. They pressed non-Amish values on us and sought to alter our perception of reality. Here is the American melting pot syndrome in action. The American way of life—both for the here and the hereafter— is the greatest in the world. All else is inferior and only the fool does not seek assimilation.

My most vivid memories of boyhood days concern hostility and harassment endured by my parents and others in the Amish community. Often "outsiders" attacked us and verbally assaulted us when we rode in our buggies. They threw firecrackers, eggs, tomatoes, even rocks. Soldiers home on leave burned our fodder shocks, overturned our outdoor toilets, broke windows and stole buggies. A favorite tactic was to sit in a car trunk and hold onto a buggy while the car sped down the road. The buggy was turned loose to smash into bits against a road bank. After witnessing many such acts of vandalism, I became terrified of non-Amishmen. My father and the other elders of the community refused to summon law officials to their defense, however. They turned the other cheek and prayed for them.

But if there was turmoil and conflict without the Amish community, peace was the watchword within its borders. We worked hard and we played hard, though without the competition of the outside world. Thrashing days, barn raisings and public auctions were a more than adequate substitute for radios, comic books and organized sports.

Amish families are close-knit. We worked as a unit for ourselves and for the Amish community. We played together. We ate together—no meal was started until all members were present, and dinner was never interrupted by Walter Cronkite. For security and love you cannot beat the Amish way of life.

Then why did I, at sixteen, make the decision to continue in school—the first step away from my Amish origins? The answer is not simple. It includes (1) a passion for knowledge and (2) a growing resentment toward my Amish heritage, sparked by the years of derision and scorn in public schools. Somewhere on my way to a Ph.D. I fulfilled the one and outgrew the other, leaving still some unanswered questions for the psychiatrists to wrestle with.

Perhaps my Amish kinsmen themselves have the best explanation: That strange world outside the Amish community claimed me. And, indeed, the campus on which I teach is a far cry from my father's farm. And "a nice black beard like your father's" I do not have. But there is no animosity, no shame, among the Amish that I have left. And though I live within mainstream society, I am also the vice-chairman of the *National Committee for Amish Religious Freedom,* the organization which defended the Amish right not to attend high school all the way to the U.S. Supreme Court and won a unanimous decision.

Preface

This book, written with deepest respect for my Amish heritage, is an attempt to reveal to the non-Amish "world" some of the genuine virtues of the Old Order Amish. The 100,000 plus Old Order, horse and buggy driving, no church house, Amish Americans have been largely overlooked by historians and social scientists. Authors who have written about the Amish generally view them as a people of great integrity and goodwill, but have often exploited their uniqueness and picturesqueness. This book is concerned with their positive, genuine values, ways and customs as observed by those best qualified—myself as a former Amish sect member and Amish children and adults who currently participate in the Amish faith.

The term "Amish," in this book, refers to the horse-and-buggy-driving, no church-house, German-speaking sect often referred to as the "plain people." No attempt has been made to write about the Mennonites, Beachy's, Black Car Amish nor other Amish offshoot groups. It should also be acknowledged that the Old Order Amish church rules vary somewhat from community to community. Thus, certain customs described herein may not necessarily apply to all Amish communities.

Although the author is no longer Amish, all other contributors to the book are currently participants of the Old Order Amish faith. The reader should bear in mind that the Amish contributors (anything which appears in **BOLD**) have not obtained formal education beyond the eighth grade as is dictated by their religion. Yet, I believe that the reader will agree that the letters, articles and short essays by the Amish are well-written, considering their first language is German!

Because the Amish oppose photos of any kind, I have chosen to have illustrations only in this book. My appreciation is extended to Sue Wittmer for doing these sketches.

To the numerous people who cooperated in the writing of this book, I owe sincere thanks. I am especially thankful to the Amish parochial school teacher who gave me the short essays and themes written by her elementary school students along with permission to use them in this book. Also, I am thankful to the editors of *Family Life*, *Blackboard Bulletin* and *Young Companion* for permitting the reprinting of the letters, editorials and short essays written by Old Order Amish people.

Joe Wittmer
Gainesville, Florida
June, 1990

Section I

Introducing the Old Order Amish

Brief Description

"I think they are beautiful people. They are so sober, The way they think, the way they feel, the way they dress—it is all one unit. They mind their own business and live their own life and I think this is beautiful."

These are the words of Mauricio Lasansky, the artist of the famous intaglio portrait, "Amish Boy," in his description of the more than 100,000 Old Order Amish people scattered throughout 20 states. Many people confuse the Old Order Amish with the Mennonites, Amana, Hutterites, Beachy's and other type religious off-shoots of the early Anabaptist. This book is about the Old Order, no-electricity, horse-and-buggy-driving Amish. Obviously, like any other culturally distinct group, the Amish may have a negative side; however, I have chosen to focus on the positive in this book.

It is difficult to pinpoint the exact number of Old Order Amish people in America today. However, we do know that 20,157 children were enrolled in Amish schools (grades one through eight) during 1989-90 (*Blackboard Bulletin*). Thus, I estimate somewhere around 100,000 living in the U.S.A. with probably another 10 or 15 thousand more living in Canada and South America.

The values of peace, total nonviolence and humility are in evidence in any Amish community. They do not teach the skills of violence and technology. An Amishman realizes early in life that he is totally non-resistant and that he will never go to war. These values, lived by the Amish adults, gain the allegiance of the Amish youth; few permanently leave the sect. Further, there is no indigence, divorce or unemployment. There is very little delinquency and no record of an Old Order Amishman being arrested for a felony and none have ever appeared on a welfare roll. The Amish also value calmness and tranquility—how can you be in a hurry while driving a horse and buggy?

Our Driving Horse

Our driver is almost red. He is a nice horse and he takes us where we want to go. Some horses kick, but old Jamie doesn't. I sit in the back of the buggy and I get scared when the cars come. They get close and make dust. Once Uncle John's got hit and the driver died. I was sad. Uncle John was hurt....

Mary, third grade

The Amish are unique and picturesque; they strive to follow the Biblical dictate to be a "peculiar people." They want no part of the values and ways that exist in the modern world about them. They wish to be left alone to live their lives away from the mainstream of the secular society. The following poem, written by a sixteen-year-old Amish female (May, 1988) depicts the tranquility of one part of the Amish way of life—that of using a horse and buggy as a mode of travel instead of a car.

A Buggy Ride

Who'd want to drive a motor car
When he could have a horse?
There may be many others who
Would take a car, of course.
They do not know the joy of it,
A horse and buggy ride.

The feel of wind upon your face,
No stuffy seat inside.
Along the road we hear birds sing.
And watch a squirrel dash,
And just enjoy the scenery
Instead of rushing past.
The sound of horses' trotting feet
Is music to the ear.
No car is ever half as nice
At any time of year.
True, winter's snows are very cold
And rain makes me quite wet.
The wind can be uncomfortable—
Our fingers freeze, and yet
I still would chose a buggy ride,
In spite of cold or heat.
I shall insist that it is true,
A buggy can't be beat.

Rhoda, Age 16

Wenger, R. Young Companion,

May, 1988, p. 21.

The Old Order Amish strive continually to remain different from the "other people," the "outsider" or the "English" as non-Amish are called. They shun the use of television, radio, telephone and most other modern technological luxuries; they travel via horse-drawn carriages. Their homes are extremely plain and lack running water, electricity, refrigerators and most other conveniences that are found in modern American homes. Their within-group conversations are in a German dialect and they wear home sewn garb reminiscent of eighteenth century Quakers. And, as a fourth grader writes, **"We don't have TV like the English do."**

No TV

I know why we don't have TV like the English do. We Amish are different like God wants. The English can have their old TV because it's not good for you. Mom and me were in Sears one day and I saw TV a bit. Mom said they use bad words and dance on TV. We didn't watch any more. I don't want TV ever in our house.

Amos, fourth grade

The first Amish came to America and settled in the William Penn colony around 1737. Twenty-one Amish arrived on the ship *Charming Nancy* on or about October 8, 1737. Three of these new arrivals were named "Miller," my mother's maiden name. However, the first "Wittmer" (Daniel) did not arrive until 1854.

History indicates that hundreds of Amish and members of other Anabaptist sects were burned at the stake or beheaded during the fifteenth and sixteenth centuries throughout Europe. The Anabaptist were especially persecuted for their rejection of infant baptism and refusal to bear arms. T*he Martyrs Mirror*, a 1,582-page book found in many Amish homes, contains a careful record of hundreds of Amish martyrs (several were named "Wittmer") and how they met their deaths. There are accounts of the severing of hands, tongues, ears and feet, plus many eyewitness accounts of crucifixions, live burials, stake-burnings and suffocations. These accounts are related over and over again to Amish children by their parents, elders and teachers. Amazingly, this past persecution has been an important element in Amish historical memories. It has helped to keep alive their present sense of distinctiveness, and has definitely contributed to their group cohesiveness.

The Old Order Amish are an austere people who live a simple agricultural life. In Europe they were considered excellent farmers and were sought after as tenants. They brought several new methods of farming with them to the William Penn colony. Every American community to which they migrated benefitted agriculturally.

The Old Order Amish have the reputation of being excellent farmers and they do all their farming with horses or mules. Although tractors may be purchased for use as belt power, the wheels will be removed and the tractor will be mounted on a wagon and pulled from job to job by horses.

A young Amish participant learns early in life that there is both an "Amish" and an "outsider" or "English" method of obtaining need satisfaction. They learn that deviant behavior results in clashes with their respective consciences and with peers and adults. Amish youth are constantly inculcated into a sense of martyrdom and realize the very real possibility of suffering at the hands of "non-believers." Parents vividly relate stories from the martyr book regarding the terrible sufferings of their forefathers. There is a pervasive tendency among all Amish to distrust the "English."

Amish History

...Our teacher told us about the early days and how other religion people hurt and killed our forefathers. They did these awful things because they would not fight in the war and would not baptize their little babies. That's why we are still called Anabaptist people. I sometimes dream about being killed because I'm Amish and it scares me....

Elam, fourth grade

The Amish sect's refusal to accept the "melting pot" concept has made them the brunt of much hostility and harassment and it is becoming increasingly more difficult for the Amish to preserve their peace-loving values in America. Many Amish feel that their simple, pious life is threatened by the turbulent society surrounding them and hundreds have immigrated to Central and South America.

Mainstream society's emphasis on high-powered cars, computers and contraceptive devices is conspicuously absent from the horse-and-buggy Amish world. The Amish constantly live by the scriptural admonitions to "Come out from among them, and be ye separate," and "Be ye a peculiar people." The Amish live in isolated communities attempting to stay apart from the secular influences of the "outsiders' world." However, the Amish feel the pressing-in of America's emphasis on technology, violence and twentieth century progress.

The New Road

The English put in a new blacktop road in our settlement. My dad thinks they should have left the old road for us or maybe some land on each side for us to drive on. Dad says horses can't run very long on blacktop and mom thinks now more tourists will come out here with cameras. I don't like the blacktop road. The cars are scary and it hurts our driver....

Samuel, fifth grade

All Amishmen are oriented toward one goal—that of eternal life. Therefore, they equate their personal pursuance of this ultimate goal with present methods of attaining it. Industry, careful stewardship, the sweat of the brow, beards on married men and German as a first language are all means to an end— eternal life. Everything they do and wear has religious significance; religion is a seven-day-a-week affair.

Uniforms of any type are taboo among the Amish and there is observable uniformity in dress. Youngsters are attired as miniature adults. There is no change in style to be concerned about and status is not attributed to the type of clothing worn. This alleviates coveting and self pride while building group cohesion. This similarity in dress also makes a deviate highly conspicuous and thus serves as a boundary-maintaining device.

Amish Clothes

...We wear plain clothes because the *Bible* says we should. Sometimes the English stare at you but they never have said anything to me about my clothes. We can be a witness for others by being plain.... I read in the last *Family Life* that just wearing plain clothes doesn't make you a Christian. I think sometimes we forget that....

Emma, seventh grade

In my former community an Amish man begins growing a chin beard the preceding week of his marriage, but the upper lip and neck are kept clean shaven. This is in keeping with their non-conformity to "worldly" values and ways as an "outsider" where a moustache is often in evidence. A straight line is shaved across the back of his neck and his hair is bobbed in a "crock-like" appearance. An Amishman does not part his hair and it is not "tapered" on the sides. The men wear large, broad-brimmed black hats, suspenders, shirts without buttons or pockets, pants without hip pockets or zippers and underwear without stripes.

All shirts are sewn in such a manner so as to necessitate being put on and removed by slipping them over the head. These are considered "orders" of the local church. Such "orders" may vary somewhat from one Amish community to another.

Amish males dress alike regardless of age—black felt hats; denim or serge trousers held up by suspenders, hooks and eyes; no shirt pockets; two-side pants pockets only and no zippers. In addition, no variance in hair style is permitted. Amish males are taught the value of hard work early in life and their lives are laid out in front of them. They will all be farmers while some will work additionally as carpenters or in closely related areas.

Something Funny

...My Dad said when he was little one time he was with my Grandpa and some English boys called them "bushhogs." Then the boys said baa-baa like a goat. I think that is funny. Dad has whiskers but nobody went baa-baa yet.

Noah, fourth grade

Amish women do not wear make-up of any sort, nor shave any part of their body. They wear dresses that are full-blown and not adorned with buttons, hooks and eyes, press buttons or zippers. The only means of keeping their dresses intact is with straight pins. They do not wear lacy under clothing and store-bought bras are prohibited. A female's hair is never cut, is always parted in the middle and is pulled tight without being "puffed up."

To an Amish person the "world" begins at the last Amish farmhouse. The Amish farmer has not acquired the "worldly" need for a tractor with which to farm. He may rely on a tractor for belt power, but it will be mounted on a steel-wheeled wagon and pulled from job to job by horses. He also uses horses to plow his fields and to pull his black buggy. Work is a moral and Biblical directive. Labor saving devices are mere temptations and "something new." Something new or different is "of the Devil" while tradition is sacred. Although stern it may seem from the outside looking in, the Amish are healthy and happy. They have not acquired the methods of the "world" to attain their happiness or to fulfill their needs. And, to the outsider, the Amish may appear shy and withdrawn. And, in the outsider's presence, they will most often appear so. However, they know how to have fun. Theirs is not a "frowning" culture as some have written.

As a former Amishman, it is difficult to explain the feeling of being truly different from the dominant, surrounding society. Amish youngsters are raised very carefully and certain methods are employed to protect them from the contaminating influences of the "outsider." The fact that they are different and peculiar is a continuous indoctrinating process for the young Amish. They develop a strong conscience and quickly learn that their behavior should always be for the good of the group. Once indoctrinated, it is indeed difficult to alter themselves to accept the values and ways of others without experiencing extreme psychic pain. Thus, those who do leave the sect (usually males between the ages of 16 and 20) often do so only temporarily. That is, they return, marry and become God-fearing members of the community again. Those who do leave the sect permanently must reject their family, their heritage and the values it represents. Psychologists agree this is seldom done without traumatic conflict for that individual. And, this inner conflict causes many to return to the fold.

Amish Origin

The Amish sect was born out of the religious turmoil of the Anabaptist movement in sixteenth century Europe. Their emergence was turbulent.

The Anabaptists were a unique group during that time in history. They were not directly involved in all the warfare taking place in the name of religion. However, they were in total disagreement with the Catholics, Luther and the Reformed movement. They wanted to return to a primitive, early-type of Christianity. To bring back this primitive Christianity, the Anabaptists literally accepted the *Bible* as their dictate. They made it clear to both church and state that they would stop taking oaths, would not drink and would never again pick up a sword. Further, they renounced all sorts of economic rewards and personal-type adornment. One of the major differences between the Anabaptists and the other religious groups at that time in history was their feeling that baptism was not to be administered in infancy, but should take place when the person was old enough to reason— when the individual had assumed responsibility for his or her soul. This return to primitive religion brought the wrath of the Reformers, the Catholics and several Protestant groups onto the Anabaptists. The Anabaptists were denounced as being heretics and were subjected to the death penalty. The previously mentioned book, *The Martyr's Mirror*, gives many detailed accounts of non-resistant Anabaptists and as to how they suffered persecution and annihilation.

Despite the tremendous suffering and death, the Anabaptists prevailed. They migrated often throughout Europe in their attempts to avoid persecution. There were the Mennonites in Holland and North Germany, the Hutterian Brethren in Moravia and the Swiss Brethren in Switzerland.

In the early 1600s a division occurred among the above mentioned Mennonite Anabaptists in Holland. In 1632 Mennonite ministers from several different areas in Europe got together in an attempt to heal the breach in the Mennonite Church in Holland. During this meeting these ministers drew up a Confession of Faith to which all present agreed. The historic meeting took place in Dort, Holland and the pact developed there is commonly known by the Amish and Mennonites today as the *Dortrecht Confession of Faith*. This original agreement had eighteen articles of faith and today, 370 years later, an Amish youth must agree to these eighteen articles of faith before he or she can be baptized into membership in the Amish church.

Article seventeen of these original eighteen articles of faith was a main factor which predetermined the founding of the Amish faith. In general, the seventeenth article of the *Dortrecht Confession of Faith* indicates that all erring members shall be "shunned." In German, this is known as the *Meidung*. Menno Simon, a former Catholic highly thought of by today's Old Order Amish, was the leader of the Anabaptists in Holland and his followers became known as "Mennists." The name "Mennonite" was later applied to the Swiss and Dutch Anabaptists. Simon observed the "shunning" of erring members and his writings can be found in many Amish homes today. However, the modern day Mennonites do not practice the *Meidung*. The *Meidung* indicates that an ex-communicated member should be avoided both physically and spiritually. This includes man and wife. The ruling bishop of the Swiss Brethren Anabaptist group did not enforce this seventeenth article. A split developed in the Church and the leader of the emerging group was an aggressive young man named Jacob Amman. (His followers became known as "Aman" which later changed to "Amish.") Amman, a Swiss Brethren bishop who lived in Canton of Bern, Switzerland, took it upon himself to excommunicate all those Swiss Brethren bishops and ministers not enforcing the *Meidung*. Thus, contrary to popular opinion, the Amish are offshoots of the more liberal Mennonites.

The practice of shunning played an important role in Amish history and the practice remains important today. However, the outside "world" knows little about shunning as it is seldom discussed or written about by the Amish or others.

The writer has (on several occasions) been a direct witness to a major aspect of shunning, that of not eating with the erring excommunicated member. The member(s) being shunned will either eat first, last or simultaneously in another room of the house. Everyone present realizes what is happening but no reference is made to the shunning and it is usually dealt with without fanfare and with little embarrassment to those shunning or to those being shunned. However, I have been present when uninformed "outsiders" have caused embarrassment. And it is always a solemn occasion and sadness prevails.

Amish Music

The songs that the Amish sing during worship service have never been placed to musical notations, and the singing is almost chant-like. The texts appear as poetry. To the uninformed outsider it must sound like mournful droning or a Gregorian chant. The songs were written during the sixteenth century by imprisoned Anabaptists, and the main theme of these old songs is of protest against wicked tyrants. The song book is known as the *Ausbund*.

The *Vorsinger* (the song leader), a male, is never selected prior to the service. Instead, the older men at the service whisper among themselves urging a certain male to begin the singing, to "lead off." However, no one wants to show pride in his singing ability and thus always declines to lead the singing on the first urging. However, with enough prodding from others, finally someone does begin (and, usually, it is the one who first declined!) In the absence of musical notations, all songs in the *Ausbund* must be learned by ear and one must be highly skilled to be the *Vorsinger*. (It also takes skill to follow his singing lead.) It takes years to learn how to sing from the *Ausbund* and seldom do males learn the songs prior to their marriage. The songs are extremely slow, and as indicated below, some may take as long as **28 minutes** to sing. Of course, this slow pace coincides well with the slow- paced Amish culture.

The following, written by an Amish person, provides a good description of Amish church singing, and as the writer points out, to be the song leader, **"can be a major undertaking."**

Singing the Old Songs

...Singing the "slow tunes" as they are sung in Amish churches today is indeed a special assignment. The Amish have kept up and handed down these tunes from generation to generation for hundreds of years. Sometime ago there was an article in *Family Life* (December, 1985) dealing with the origin of Amish church tunes. This article pointed out that although they may be distantly related to the Gregorian chants, they belong in a class of their own.

Why do we sing in church? Is it to keep the congregation occupied while the ministers are conferring in the *"Abrote?"* Hardly! We believe it serves a necessary purpose. A farmer would not think of sowing his seed without first getting the soil in shape. Singing these old hymns can be likened to the final harrowing before planting the crop. It should help in getting our minds into a prayerful receptive mood. What could be a better way to do this than to actively join in singing these hymns?

Indications are that this type of music grew out of the early Anabaptist church music. Without beat or measure, time or rhythm, it depends upon depth and devotion, appealing to the nobler sentiments of the heart such as reverence, faith and a prayerful attitude. Appreciation for this type of music must be learned, but once its value is perceived, it will be highly esteemed.

To a person not used to singing this type of music, the first difference he will notice is that the song leader sings the first syllable of each line alone. Since there are normally 2 to 5 notes to each syllable, this can be a major undertaking, especially if he is not too well acquainted with the song (p. 13).

Joe Wittmer, Ph.D.

...If you are asked to lead a song in a strange community you may be concerned because you do not know how fast they sing. This is of little importance as it will be expected that you will probably sing like you are used to at home.

Actually the one leading the song has but little effect on how long it takes to sing a song. Each community has its own pattern and there is very little variation in the length of time it takes to sing a song, regardless of who is leading.

It is always interesting to me to note how long it takes to sing *Das Loblied*. Twenty minutes is about the normal time for most Amish communities. For some of the plainer churches it takes 24 minutes and Swartzentruber groups may take up to 28 minutes.

Whatever it is in your community, it will vary very little from Sunday to Sunday...(p. 16).

Wagler, D., *Family Life*, July, 1988

Jacob Amman also introduced communion services twice a year instead of the usual once a year observed by the Swiss Brethren. Further, he introduced the communion practice still held today by the Old Order Amish, that of foot washing. Amman introduced uniformity in all forms of dress. He further taught that it was sinful to trim the beard. All of these practices are observed among today's Old Order Amish. The Amman group (later known as Amish) and the Swiss Brethren Group attempted reconciliation at least twice but to no avail. The animosity between the groups was such that even as they left Switzerland together for America they refused to ride in the same boat. This gap, which began over three hundred years ago, still exists today (to a certain extent) between the Amish and the Mennonites.[1]

---

[1] Parts of this section first appeared in Wittmer, J. (1988). Old order Amish: Culturallly different by religion. In Vacc, N., Wittmer, J., and DeVaney, S., *Experiencing and Counseling Multicultural and Diverse Populations*. Muncie, IN: Accelerated Development, Inc.

Section II

The Amish Family System

Married-Pair Living

The family system is the primary unit which organizes the dominant patterns of value orientation within the Old Order Amish culture. In most all societies it is in the family where basic normative evaluations are developed. It is the older members of the family, among the Amish particularly, that funnel the cultural heritage to the younger offspring. It is their solemn duty. It is in the Amish family setting that the child first learns to respond to authority, to play roles in the cooperative structure, and to obey the norms of the sect.

Rank differences are not extreme within Amish society nor within the family structure. However, father commands the highest rank with mother being second. Sibling rank is based according to age. The older siblings often discipline the younger children, both verbally and physically.

The Amish family organization is strictly patriarchal. The Amish father raises his son in the exact manner as he was reared by his father. The father-son relationship is of a high caliber and the generation gap seldom exists. The women of the family take a back seat to the men in most endeavors and the Amish male rarely does the tasks of a female. However, women are expected to help with most male tasks. Only on special occasions such as butchering, cooking apple butter and weddings does the husband participate in household tasks. However, women and adolescent girls frequently help with the harvest of crops, especially during cornhusking, shucking wheat and so forth.

Amish married couples never show overt affection for one another in public. The Amish man refers to his wife as "her" and she makes reference to "him." However, there is mutual respect and seldom does arguing occur in front of the children.

Although there are varying degrees of cooperation between the husband and wife in fulfillment of their roles, the Amish generally adhere to the Biblical tradition in which the husband is in direct charge over both his wife and his children. Male and female roles are clearly differentiated and the woman's place is perhaps best typified by the Biblical admonition that "the head of the woman is the man."

Young Amish females know that their adult role will be that of a farmer's wife and they are taught the skills of cooking, canning and other related "housewife" chores early in life. And, in the absence of electricity and refrigeration, this is no easy task. Although they may be teachers in Amish schools for a few years, they will never hold positions in the church or elsewhere and they know that, as the Bible dictates, "The head of the woman is the man."

The following article, written by an Amish male back in 1971 and reprinted in part here, gives the Biblical justification for the distinct role differentiation found in the Amish family structure. And, it is my opinion that the following accurately portrays the way things are today among the Amish.

Men and Women

...In many ways the world is a man's world. Men have the advantage when it comes to the highest paying jobs, making the big decisions, of running for president. The odds are in their favor when a ranch manager is being hired. Most of the top positions in business and government are held by men.

Perhaps it is true that men have not always been as nice and as fair to women as they should have been. I'm sure they haven't. Some men have looked down upon women with scorn, as if they were an inferior kind of human. Even today in many countries, women are trodden down and misused by their husbands as if they were their slaves, or a piece of personal property.

Such an overbearing attitude is wrong. But is it any more wrong than the modern movement by women who no longer are submissive to their husbands, who want to get into roles for which God never intended them? Which extreme is more wrong? I don't think there is any difference. Neither is right.

It is not surprising that non-Christian women go on a campaign to assert what they think are their rights as humans. Without the teaching of the *Bible*, they have no guide to know what is God's intended order between the sexes. Their reasoning is that a person is a person, therefore why make a difference in any way?

But those of us who read the *Bible* should make our decisions by the Word of God, and not by human reasoning. Yet it is a sad fact that churches are strongly influenced by what goes on outside. Sometimes the influence of the world seems to be stronger than the influence of the *Bible*.

...Peter, in his first epistle, says that wives should be subject to their husbands, even if their husbands are unbelievers. What better way to win a husband to the faith than by humbly staying in her place? Matthew Henry comments on the third chapter of 1 Peter, "A Cheerful subjection, and a loving reverential respect, are duties which Christian women owe their husbands whether they be good or bad.... The subjection of wives to their husbands is a duty which has been practiced universally by holy women in all ages."

...These verses leave no room for misunderstanding. Man is to be the head of the woman. Since this is the case, it would not seem proper to have women in positions of authority where they would rule over men. This the Apostle teaches, "Let the women learn in silence with all subjection. But I suffer not a woman to teach, nor to usurp authority over the man, but to be in silence" (I Tim. 2:11-12). To the Corinthians Paul wrote much the same thing, "Let your women keep silence in the churches; for it is not permitted unto them to speak; but they are commanded to be under obedience, as also saith the law. And if they will learn anything, let them ask their husbands at home: for it is a shame for women to speak in the church."

...So far we have chosen Scripture passages that speak to women, that command them to be submissive to their husbands and respect God's order. What about the husbands? If they are to rule the household, does this mean God has appointed them to be dictators, and their word to be law? Hardly. Instead, the verses in the *New Testament* that are directed to husbands instruct them to love their wives and to treat them with courtesy and respect.

The whole world has a distaste of the woman who henpecks her husband, the wife who is determined to "wear the pants in the family." All of us have seen examples of the disharmony that can result when husbands and wives get mixed up in their roles—when the wife is the boss, and the husband is in subjection to her.

When things get out of their proper order—when women usurp authority either in the family or in the church—it is a sad situation. And yet, is it not true that the blame often comes right back to the husband, or in the case of the church, to its leaders? In many such cases the husband has failed to fill his role as the head of the home, or the church leaders have failed to hold up a Biblical standard. When man's leadership breaks down, it is no wonder that the woman steps in.

Recently, as I was reading Dr. Spock's *Baby and Child Care*, I was startled again and again by the fact that in the world today, the mother trains the children. She is the disciplinarian and she makes the decisions. In the book, the author directs his advice to the mother. It gave me the impression that the father is the bread-earner, but as a member of the family he just doesn't exist.

Why has the modern mother become the head of the family? I fear it is largely because Father has failed to fill the position.

...Is a woman a lesser person because she is ordained of God to be in subjection to man? Is it a misfortune to be born a girl? I am positive the answer to these questions is a strong, "No!" Yet many rebellious women would disagree with me.

Is it such a strange thing that God should ask women to be subject to men? Not at all. No one, female or male, can escape authority. From childhood, we are subject to our parents. Paul writes to the Romans, "Let every soul be subject unto the higher powers (governments)." Concerning the ministers of the church, we are commanded, "Obey them that have the rule over you, and submit yourselves."

...Life is full of authority. Being a woman means there is one more level of subjection than being a man. That is all. It doesn't mean that a woman is thereby being degraded, cheated or despised. It is simply a fact of life, like being born a girl in the first place.

> Life is just as happy and just as meaningful for one sex as the other. The secret is in fulfilling one's God-given role. For most women this means being a wife and mother—a homemaker and a help mate. Many unmarried sisters find fulfillment teaching school, helping the needy or caring for invalid relatives.
>
> Stoll, J., *Family Life*, October, 1971.

Farms are usually jointly owned in order to secure legal ownership in the case of death. And property, whether farm land and equipment or household goods, are generally spoken of as "ours." However, transactions involving sale or purchase are made through the husband or have his approval. However, the husband and wife usually confer before making any large purchases.

The single woman, as well as the single man, lacks status in the family-oriented community. A bachelor cannot hold church office and a spinster can look forward to a lifetime of doing other people's housework or taking in sewing. Recently, some single Amish women have begun working in hospitals, factories and stores.

A wife may get to keep the egg money for household expenses if she takes care of the chickens, but more often the money is doled out by her husband as she needs it.

Convenience foods are not purchased by the average Amish housewife. She plants a large garden and cans hundreds of quarts of fruits and vegetables for the winter. There is no freezing of food.

The wife also has responsibility for the appearance of the lawn and area surrounding the house, including the whitewashing of fences, posts and grape arbors in the Spring.

Gardening, except for the initial spading or plowing in the Spring, is the sole responsibility of the wife. There is usually a large variety of vegetables which always includes cucumbers and red beets—standard items served at the luncheon given during the Sunday services (held in private homes).

Another area which requires a large part of the wife's time is the processing of fruits and vegetables in the summer and meats in the winter. In the absence of refrigeration, this takes unique skills and much time.

Amish women are known as good cooks and the Amish people eat well, usually with an abundance of food. Breakfast usually consists of eggs, fried cornmeal mush, liverwurst, cooked cereal and fried potatoes. No meal is without bread, butter and apple butter. The typical diet is rich in fats and carbohydrates with potatoes, gravy, fried foods and pastries.

Becoming a Housewife

...Someday, I know I will be a housewife and I look forward to it. Being a housewife will be my full-time job. Mom told me that "English" women have other jobs. Not me. I'm going to be a housewife and be a good wife for my husband....

Delilah, fourth grade

Along with preparing the meals, the Amish wife makes all the clothes of the family. Yard goods, usually denim, serge, gabardine and organdy, are purchased in a nearby town for this purpose.

Men are considered more able to perform duties in public affairs and similarly women are usually silent during the progress of religious practices and ceremonies. Women never serve as church officials, on school boards and so forth.

The bulk of the husband's duties, of course, center around the production of farm products for market. The Amish farmer is known by the crops he produces. The uniformity of dress and lifestyle of Amish families make differentiation on almost any other basis impossible. However, even these distinctions are undercut by the religious emphasis on humility and the sinfulness of pride. An Amish farmer faces excommunication if he shows undue pride in his dairy herd or other possessions.

How does the Amish wife feel about her role? The following small piece written by an Amish wife best describes, I believe, the feeling of the majority.

Helping My Husband

A father really is someone. It is a serious business to be a father for God expects great things of the man. When a man marries, he must accept the obligations and responsibilities for the physical, moral and spiritual welfare of his home. God intends for the man to set the pattern for his children.

The woman is the weaker vessel and it is her duty to be the keeper of the home. A wife who tries to help her husband in every way will receive many blessings beyond measure. She must trust her husband's judgment and stand back of him.

A father is someone who needs to be feared, not as one who rules with an iron rod. It is for our protection that we obey him and respect his judgment.

After John became my husband, his life was never quite the same. God said when a man and woman marry, they shall leave father and mother and the two shall be one flesh. Few people really realize what all this includes. The husband is the provider, the protector, the delivered of his wife's body. Every man who marries takes care of his wife as a sacred trust. The husband is to be the head of the home, even as Christ is of the church. As the church is obedient to Christ so shall the wife be to her husband.

It seems at our house things don't go as smoothly when Dad is not around. There always seems to be more tension and frustrations, but when he is here, everyone feels a sense of security and protection and everything goes better. When a storm comes up, I always feel better when my husband is at home with me and the children.

At first John worked away from home but this never seemed right. The children and I would do the chores by ourselves. I remember the evening when John said, "Wouldn't it be nice to milk more cows and make our living off the farm?"

I have often thanked the Lord for letting me marry a farmer, for there are many blessings in a farm home. A faithful wife can encourage a farmer a great deal. The investment needed to start farming can frighten a man whose wife is a spendthrift.

The father is the provider and the bread earner but the wife and children need to help all they can in the duties and labors of a home. A father should talk financial problems over with his wife. The children ought to listen in for children can often learn a lot by just listening. A lot less problems come up in homes where the husband can talk with his wife in a loving way, and where the father enjoys the children.

God expects the man to take the lead for the woman is the weaker vessel. It is her duty to make a home out of a house, where her husband can come home to meet his love, not a grouch!

There must be love between husband and wife. Remember you were each other's choice and this was your answer to a lonely heart and to supply the comfort and joy of fellowship. When two walk together, life is much happier. If one stumbles, the other is there to hold him up. If one is discouraged, the other one should give encouragement. Two people can sleep warmer than one. Two hearts can be more cheerful and happy than either one alone. Happiness in married life is something that has to be worked for, it will not come naturally.

What can be lovelier and more beautiful than a home where husband and wife and children work together for the spiritual welfare of each other?

Anonymous—Reprinted from *Family Life*

To my knowledge, divorce is non-existent. And there are no written or unwritten provisions for securing either a divorce or a separation. Marriage is supported by kinship and religious sanction. Although Amish couples do not reveal any overt signs of affection for one another when in public, they most certainly do in private. Although the notion of procreation may be upper most in their minds, it is the opinion of the writer that Amish couples do have very satisfactory intimate relationships.

Most Amish couples have several children and they realize that when they grow old the children will care for them. It is nice to grow old Amish. The older you get, the wiser you become and your future does not include a nursing home. The youngest son brings his bride to his parents farm. At this time, a second residence is usually built for the parents a short distance away—the old folks get the new homes in the Amish community. The management of the farm is then turned over to the son, and the parents retire. Relationships between the two families are cordial, and even the mother-in-law/daughter-in-law relationship, which is so troublesome for other cultures with patriarchal family customs, seems to be quite amicable.

In summary, once married, an Amish woman expects no public expressions or gestures of affection from her husband. She works with him to make a good life for them and their children and to gain the respect of the community. She does not have to work to keep him. Marriage is for keeps and a roving eye is not tolerated by the community.

Children and Growing Up

Amish couples do not practice birth control and pray for children. It is indeed a happy occasion when a child is born to Amish parents. A new baby is showered with love and neighbors come from miles around for "sweet coffee." "Sweet coffee" is the term, in the writer's former Amish community, given to the custom of visiting and eating at the home of the grateful Amish parents. There are no Godfather ceremonies nor gifts.

In the following letter, an Amish lady best describes the Amish people's feelings concerning birth control.

The Amish are recognized as expert horsemen and provide their animals with excellent care. "Drivers," those horses bred for pulling buggies, are pampered and cared for especially well. Blacktop and concrete roads dictate that "drivers" be fitted with metal shoes. Although some Amish men are more expert than others, all males are taught the skill of "horseshoeing" at a young age.

The Pill

...in these times some may be tempted not to have a family or limit the size. Read Genesis 38:9. The pill, I would say, is not pleasing to God who has made us pure and holy. Paul writes that young women should marry, bear children and guide the house.

Anonymous— Reprinted from *Family Life*

This writer has never known a time when the birth of a child was an unwelcomed event in the Amish community. A baby means another corn husker, another cow-milker, but, most of all, another God-fearing Amishman. The birth is always seen as a blessing of the Lord. Thus, Amish parents feel that their children really do not belong to them. As the Amish mother in the following piece indicates, **"I have no children,"** they belong to God.

I Have No Children

I am a young mother and our house rings with merry voices and childish laughter. However, I have no children. God has given us on loan, two precious souls to nurture and cherish for a period of time to fit them for the Kingdom.

If these were MY children, I would love them so much I could not bear to punish them. I would overlook their childish tantrums and if they should strike me while angry, I would smile indulgently. But because these children belong to the Lord, and I am His servant, I will punish them when necessary. Whom the Lord loveth, He chasteneth, and can His servants do less? Also, because His word warns that children should obey and respect their parents (Eph. 6:1), I will not permit a child to strike at me jokingly, much less in anger.

If these were MY children I would want to dress them attractively to draw attention to the natural beauty which God has blessed them with. However, because these are God's children and His word refers often to the dress of immoral women, (Prov. 7:10), I will dress them modestly when they are small, so that as they reach the age of accountability, they will not be strangers to God's standard of dress. First of all I will hold forth this standards in my own life, (I Tim. 2:9) because God has blessed me with hands to sew and I cannot blame my dress standard on others.

If these children belonged to ME I would want to send them to the best schools, have them read all the current best sellers, regardless of content, and in every way fit them to obtain good jobs and live a life of ease. But since these are God's children, and if the Lord tarries till they are of school age, I will send them to a Christian day school to help fit them for eternity, and trust God to lead them when school years are past.

If these were MY children as they enter their teen years, I would provide them with all the "extras," a car, radio, television and the latest fashionable clothes, so that they would be invited to the best places, date the most prominent people and in general "live it up" before settling down to earn a living. But since these are God's children, I will, with His help, admonish them and teach them by word and by example that God commands us to abstain from the unequal yoke. Also, together we will read and strive to obey Titus, Chapter 2, for this is God's order for our life. At no time will I give the impression that the teen years are for foolishness and seeking pleasure, but rather for seeking God's will for our adult life. I will try to impress upon them that "What a man sows, that must he also reap."

If these were MY children and I followed my own selfish desires for their life I would share with them as much as possible in enjoying the worldly pleasures and in seeking after such. I would also spend with them an endless eternity in the torments of hell and I would be largely responsible as their mother for influencing them in that direction. After it is too late we would see that a life lived for self and things done for the glory of man have their reward in eternal suffering.

However, because these are God's children, and I have renounced self and seek to obey my husband as he obeys God, we, through the grace of God and the keeping power of our Lord Jesus Christ, will share the joys of Heaven throughout the ceaseless ages of eternity, to Him be all honor, praise and glory.

Anonymous—Reprinted from Family Life

The Amish are a fertile group and very few couples are without offspring. Families usually range from eight to ten children. There were two Amish families in my community with 15 natural children. Couples without children are a rarity and childless couples often adopt non-Amish babies. The latter has caused consternation among some "local" uninformed outsiders.

My Baby Brother

Noah was born last Tuesday and our family is excited. We are now a family of 5 boys and 5 girls. Noah is tiny and red but dad says he will grow up to be a good farmer like all my brothers and me....

Yost, fifth grade

Today more and more Amish children are being delivered in local hospitals; however, most are still delivered at home, as was the writer, by an Amish midwife. Sometimes, as in my case, someone forgets to record the birth with local officials. Thanks to carefully kept records in the family *Bible*, I obtained a valid birth certificate when entering high school.

My contacts with MDs from Amish communities and with Amish mid-wives indicate that Amish women generally have an easy time in having their children. It is unknown where the mid-wife receives her training, but I assume it is through observation. I was never present in the room where children were delivered. However, I remember, on at least one occasion, carrying the boiling water to the entrance of the room where my older sister was delivering. In this case, the midwife, my stepmother and the new mother's husband were the only ones present in the room where the delivery occurred.

Non-Amish people marvel at the attention, the love and the affection given to the newborn infant. Even when asleep the infant will often be in someone's arms. For the first several months of life he or she will be held almost constantly by some member of the family. It is the custom to take the baby with them wherever the parents go, even to the fields to work. And, the baby will also attend the long church services when just a few weeks old.

The Amish baby is a pleasure and a gift of God who is too precious to be left in a nursery or with a baby sitter. A baby is an integral part of the family from the moment of birth. The attention and love given to the baby is difficult to describe; you almost have to observe it to understand its significance.

There may be such a thing as a spoiled baby; however, Amish parents seldom refer to an infant as being spoiled. Matter of fact, an infant can do no wrong, they remain blameless. If adjustment problems occur, the parents and community erred.

As previously mentioned, an Amish baby receives much attention and affection. For example, an Amish baby is not diapered on some cold table. This activity is carried out on someone's lap, usually the mother or an older sister.

Amish parents seldom read the books on how to raise children and they do not stick to strict time schedules and so forth. If a baby cries, something is wrong, and if hungry, he or she is fed regardless of the hour.

Food from the table is shared with the baby at a very early age. It is not unusual to see a four month-old baby being fed mashed potatoes directly from the table while sitting in the mother's lap. Eating is a very important activity for an Amish family and they feel that one always eats better in a group. Eating is a family affair which includes the baby.

To an outsider it may appear that the Amish mother is hiding her infant from the eyes of the world when she is in public. The baby is almost always covered in its entirety with a blanket. Amish women always wear a black shawl over their shoulders and many times it is almost impossible to realize that the mother is carrying a baby. She will have the baby carefully tucked away under her shawl. I once asked a late aunt about this custom and she indicated that the Amish child should be protected, at an early age, from the "world."

Every Amish baby, if physically possible, is breast fed. I do not feel that any turmoil exists in the Amish culture concerning whether to breast feed or not to. It is simply the only thing to do. Breasts are not seen as sex symbols and feeding may take place anywhere at any time, as no apparent shame or humility is attached to breast feeding in public. This should not be construed to mean that breast feeding will take place in a local department store. However, when Amish are gathered socially, or in church, breast feeding takes place without any apparent shame. As the following Amish lady's letter indicates, it is seen as being very natural.

Breast Feeding

...I am a believer in nature as part of God's creation. The plain people are becoming somewhat indifferent as to what used to be the rule for mothers in the past. In Lamentations 2:3 we can read, "The daughter of my people is become cruel, like the ostriches in the wilderness." I have heard that the hen ostrich cares very little for her nest or her offspring. The male cares for them nights which is quite the reverse for most all other creatures.

"The tongue of the sucking child cleaveth to the roof of his mouth for thirst" (Lam. 4:4). I once read a doctor's article that dealt close to nature. He remarked that the invention of the bottle has been the greatest single cause of colic.

Man is also given an example in nature. Even the sea monsters draw out the breast. They give suck to their young ones. (This is their life).

> This is not meant to offend anyone, but it says not "my people" but "the daughter of my people." It may seem incorrect to say, "Thy will be done" when no effort is made to use members in the way God intended.
>
> Anonymous—Reprinted from *Family Life*

Another aspect of Amish child rearing which is uncommon to the "outsider" culture is the fact that the new baby often sleeps with his or her parents for the first few months of life. Along with the security this practice affords, it is also convenient for breast feeding and provides warmth. Psychologically, this practice may contribute more to the Amish youths' apparent security than any other factor. It is difficult to pinpoint the age at which weaning occurs. However, contrary to medical fact, many Amish still believe that the longer they nurse the less is the chance of another pregnancy and thus Amish babies usually nurse longer than babies of the "outsider" culture. Breast feeding is viewed as a natural form of birth control.

Toilet training usually begins around age two with no apparent harshness or anxiety attached to the endeavor. As previously stated, Amish babies are held almost constantly, and of course, in the absence of rubber pants or snap on diapers (which are considered "worldly") they often leave their "mark" on the holder's lap. This may draw a snicker from an "outsider" observer; however, the wet spot warrants no attention or concern from the Amish people present. In the absence of modern, closed-in bathrooms, waste containers for human elimination (these are usually gray or white porcelain) are evident in Amish bedrooms. To the Amish, human elimination is simply a natural activity and thus toilet training is facilitated by the process of imitation and observation. This should not be construed to mean that there is no privacy; however, there is much less concern over privacy associated with this endeavor than in the "outsider" culture. Bedroom doors are not fitted with locks.

Amish parents believe that one of their basic duties is to transmit the Amish cultural heritage to their children. They are not alone in this high priority activity as the total Amish community is highly involved in the rearing of all its participants. However, as in any culture, child rearing is not taken lightly. Some Amish parents provide some rules for raising children in the following essay written for *Family Life*.

Things To Do BEFORE Your Children Grow Up

Train up a child in the way he should go, and when he is old, he will not depart from it (Proverbs 22:6).

"These words, which I command thee shall be in thine heart and thou shalt teach them diligently unto thy children, and shalt talk of them when thou sittest in thine house and when thou walkest by the way and when thou liest down, and when thou risest up" (Deut. 22:5-6)

We must be by example what we want our children to be. Children are great imitators. Your example is of utmost importance.

Be a parent, not just a playmate, but do play and pray together. If you love your children, then let *idleness* be counted as a sin in your family.

Be sure you have confidence in your children and they in you.

Let them know you are for them and not against them.

Be as good as your word if you want them to be as good as their word.

Work along with your children in their work and take an interest in what they do, or they may lose interest in what they do.

Pray for your children. The genuineness of your prayers will teach them the reality of God.

Devotions should not be merely an instruction period, but rather adoration, praise, love and appreciation of God.

Songs of praise magnify the wonders of God.

When conditions are as they should be in the home, it is a foretaste of Heaven.

As fathers and mothers, grandfathers and grand-mothers, we have the biggest job in the world to teach our children to love the Lord.

Disobedience and disrespect for parents are often the first steps downward that children take.

No man who dishonors father or mother ever prospers in the long run.

Isaac was so holy before his children, that when Jacob remembered God, he remembered him in the "fear of his father Isaac" (Gen. 31:53).

When parents err in their judgment and later recognize and confess it, they gain the respect of the child.

Unity between parents is a must. When one parent says something, the other should back him up.

Study your *Bible*: acquaint your children with the simple truths of the Word.

There must be much gentleness and patience along with instructions, "lest they become discouraged" (Col. 3:21).

It always pays to speak kindly, and especially to husband, wife or children.

If parents want the gratitude of their children, let them talk to them as though they were human beings. "Like begets like."

Love produces love and hatred reproduces hatred. It is usually the scolding parents who are disrespected by their children. Reproofs should always be given in gentle tones.

These do not belong in a Christian home: slang, vulgarity, frivolity, uncourteous treatment of youngsters, disrespect for elders, talking back to parents.

Never compare your child with other children. If you compare them favorably, they may become proud, if unfavorably, discouraged.

As soon as children show anger, they are old enough to be punished. A child will not desire to touch a hot stove more than once or twice. Our discipline should follow the same pattern.

A child is not trained properly until he obeys when told the first time, without question, and without need for the parent to raise his voice.

Use discipline to correct your child, be fair but be firm.

Mother shall help faithfully, but Father must shoulder the blame if training of the children is not accomplished.

If the woman has the lead in the conversation too much in the home, it is evidence that she is out of God's order: Christ, man, and then woman.

In the sight of God it is much better for the woman to be of a meek and quiet spirit (I Peter 3:3-4).

Demanding obedience to satisfy every selfish whim or acting like a slave driver without due respect for the children, cannot be tolerated in the Christian home. Children will quickly discern whether or not we mean what we say.

When children are old enough to understand, they should be taught the basic facts about sex and the reproduction of life before they learn it from a perverted source in an unscriptural manner.

Young people may develop sinful habits because they are not aware of the meaning of the impulses within them. A knowledge of the facts of life can help them from getting into habits which may trouble them for life.

Buying everything he wants results in a spoiled child. The parents should know what is best for the children.

When our children leave for school and other places, do we send them off with a smile and a pleasant farewell?

A child can read a parent's character before he can read the alphabet.

You can't pull the wool over the children's eyes so the best way to teach the Gospel is to live it.

When childhood closes, life's training is mostly done.

Children have only one childhood. We can fail in business and often times start over and make good. But if we fail in the teaching and training of our children, we never get another chance.

To be really effective in training up a child in the way he should go, we must be sure that we travel that road ourselves first.

— *Compiled by Amish parents who have a concern for the on-coming generation.*

Anonymous—Reprinted from *Family Life*

At approximately the age of two, restrictions and exacting disciplines have already begun to be continually imposed on the Amish child. Amish parents inform their children at a very young age why they cannot have store-bought "worldly" clothes, bicycles and other type toys like those of the children who live outside the Amish community. They are given sound Biblical reasons as to why their family cannot have electricity, cars, radios, televisions and comic books. Amish children are taught that they should remain separate and different from the strange and fearful "outsider" world.

Amish children are taught to speak in German and Amish parents do not want anyone speaking English to their infants. The learning of English comes at a later time; just previous to entering the first grade. A four- or five-year-old Amish child seldom understands or speaks English.

Amish youth are taught respect for those in authority. They will learn to enjoy work and to fulfill their responsibilities. The obedience expected from Amish children is not based on strict authority but instead is based on love and the belief that those in authority truly have the concern for them. By this I mean that you soon learn that those in authority care about what happens to you more than they care about themselves. Thus, if your parents have taught you right from wrong, to do wrong would be to let them down and show your lack of concern for their feelings. You learn through a gradual process of indoctrination to be truly concerned with the feelings of those around you and especially the feelings of those in authority. This brings about humbleness and guilt feelings when you let these people down by doing "wrong." Although the "outsider" may view this method of child rearing as being harsh, this writer can remember only one "light" physical punishment during his entire time at home. My father used to indicate that the guilt over the concern of hurting others was enough punishment. There may be considerable variation among the Amish communities as to how disobedience is handled. However, it is my estimation that there are fewer physical confrontations between the youth and those in authority than one is led to believe.

The rights of the Amish parents over the children are great. It can be observed that Amish children obey and respect their parents and very little of the children's behavior is irrelevant to the parents, especially their father. He feels justified in observing the Biblical right to influence most of their actions. It is evident that the Amish wife and children are submissive to him, but his values tell the Amish father that he has the cultural and Biblical responsibility to run the family. The Amish father does initiate the action in the family, but the rarity of arbitrary decisions on his part is impressive.

Some "outsiders" may feel that the value orientation patterns prescribed for the Amish children will accomplish social conformity at the expense of curiosity and fantasies about the "real world." This is the desire of Amish parents. And, in the absence of newspapers, books, fairy tales, radio, television and creative surroundings, the Amish youth's imagination and creativity are at a minimum. Yet, Amish youth appear to be happy and satisfied with their life as it is and feel very insecure when away from home and community.

Much emphasis is placed on teaching the young Amish child the value of sharing. If there is a smaller baby or infant the pre-schooler will be taught how to care for the child; helping to tie shoes and so forth. Older children can often be observed in helping their younger siblings put on shoes, coats, boots and other articles of clothing. Although the younger child may be able to accomplish these tasks alone, he or she may wait for the assistance of an older sibling. My late father (as do other Amish) felt that being given the opportunity to help someone you cared for strengthened the bond between you.

Two Special Sisters

I like to help my mother in the house. I help her take care of my two little sisters. They are on a special diet. They can't have cake or pie, just special cookies. They can only have potatoes, green beans and some other vegetables, but not many of them. All their food has to be weighed. They are not allowed to have flour, milk or eggs. We bake some cookies with a special wheat starch, and use artificial milk for their cereal, which must also be in small amounts and weighed.

My one sister cannot help herself very well, but she can talk and is very pleasant to care for.

I have other sisters, too. We all help each other care for our little sisters. There is always plenty of work to do.

I am thankful for the many blessings we have.

Grade 5, Age 11, Reprinted from *Family Life*

Amish parents believe that a young child does not know the difference between right and wrong. The child was born without sin and is blameless. Thus, it is their duty to teach their children the difference between right and wrong so that they will choose the correct way of the Amish culture. Temper tantrums, making faces, name calling and so forth among Amish youngsters are extremely rare. Amish children are taught humility and to obey. This can readily be observed at the table as Amish youth speak only when spoken to. Fighting and quarreling among siblings and peers is at a minimum. As mentioned above, sibling members learn to share and it is common to see several brothers and sisters eating from the same school lunch bucket at an Amish parochial school. There is very little conflict among Amish family members. Amish youngsters are taught to settle their differences by talking to the person with whom they differ. Should two adult Amishmen come into conflict, both bring two other Amishmen with them to a meeting where the six settle the differences. Amish youngsters learn to imitate their parents and do not observe cowboys on television settling their differences with guns!

Amish children do not receive an allowance. Should the parents take a child along to town, he or she may be given a small sum of money with which to buy candy. It is strictly taboo to spend money on Sunday and in any manner for individual recreation. However, sometimes a family will visit a zoo or a similar place. Should some of the sons or daughters "hire out" for a few days, any money earned by them would automatically be turned over to their father. This continues until the youth reaches the age of 21 or marries, whichever comes first. The Amish family is often described as an economic model that teaches its children thriftiness. Amish fathers are known to be *extremely* parsimonious. This value pattern is transmitted from parents to offspring by imitation and observation.

Special significance to family interaction and value patterns can be observed at the family table. The whole family gathers here three times a day for family discussions and spiritual devotion. During the family meals the value patterns of the family and community are overtly evident. A meal is not eaten without all existing family members being present; and lateness to the table is not tolerated. Each family member has an assigned seating place at the table. This place at the table becomes symbolic of belonging to the family and is evidence of family solidarity. When this place is vacated by death, by marriage, by father having gone to town or by discipline of the *Meidung*, it becomes a subject of deep concern.

Silent prayers are said before and after the meal. No one excuses him or herself from the table until the final silent prayer is observed. To memorize and recite a prayer would be evidence of self pride and would be contrary to the prescribed value of humility. (All family prayers, during morning and evening devotional periods, are read from prayer books. Reading occurs even though it is obvious that the father, down through the years, has memorized the prayer. The same prayer is read each devotional period. The entire family is on its knees in unison.)

Talking at the table is not encouraged for the sake of conversation. Mealtime becomes the time for expressing likes and dislikes, discussing the prescribed values of the family and community, discussing work to be done and decision making.

The Amish believe their actions to be more important than their reflections or thinking. This can best be observed by the parents' lack of teaching the "outsiders'" common courtesies of "pardon me" and so forth to their children. An Amishman's loud "belch" following dinner is more of an indication to the cook that he enjoyed the meal than saying "thank you." It is seldom that anyone asks another to pass the food that he himself can reach, everyone reaches and helps himself in an orderly manner. It is a tradition, following the pre-meal prayers, for the Amish father to state, "Reach and help yourself." It is also uncommon for an Amishman to knock on another Amishman's door before entering his home. And dinner guests often drop in at the last minute without a previous invitation. They teach that actions of kindness are much more important than mere words or money. This was in evidence several years ago when several bus loads of adult males from an Amish community in Pennsylvania traveled to Mississippi at their own expense to assist non-Amish following hurricane Camile. Also, the Amish farmer does not believe in the "outsider's" method of "social security" and is exempt from paying it. He knows his neighbors will be there when he needs them. And they do not send money to feed the poor in India, for example, they will have a community "butchering" and send several thousand cans of "home-canned" beef or pork. When Amish gather in mass to help someone it is called a "frolic" and almost always ends with homemade ice cream for all. A ten-year-old Amish boy writes about such a "frolic" in the following essay in the *Blackboard Bulletin*.

A Field of Corn

Last spring the parents of our school decided to plant a field of corn. It was a 17-acre field, and the corn was planted to help pay for our schoolhouse. One day a frolic was made to plow the field. They had the plowing done in one day. Then the parents of the school planted the corn and took care of it.

Then on October 28, another frolic was held in this corn field. The men, women and children got together to help husk the corn. Some of the women made dinner.

The husking was done by 4:00. We had ice cream in the afternoon.

Grade 4, Age 10

Anonymous—Reprinted from the *Blackboard Bulletin*

Family group participation in recreation is at a minimum. As previously stated, spending money for any type of recreation is strictly taboo. This includes the purchase of any type of recreational equipment for the home and any forms of enjoyment for the family must be home-made and simple. Young girls find pleasure in clapping games while boys enjoy playing with a home-made checker set or going hunting. Weekly auctions, a favorite pastime, or visiting relatives, eating supper with friends, threshing meetings, husking bees, barn raisings, frolics of all sorts and weddings take up much of the leisure time of both children and adults.

The home is extremely important to the Amish family. It is in the home where you are born, go to church, get married and where your funeral will be held. In the essay below, an Old Order Amish person writes about the home and the importance of keeping it simple. As with most short essays in *Family Life*, this one is unsigned, but it is definitely a female writer and, I feel that the reader will agree that she paints a beautiful picture of the simple Amish family life.

I Am Rich

Home is a place to relax. It need not be a fancy structure or modern. It is not just a place to eat and sleep and change clothes like a filling station. It can be a harbor of peace—if the Lord is permitted inside.

In our home we have no running water. A pump at the kitchen sink furnishes all the water we care to use. We have no skin problems for with our silky rain water, we need no detergents. When getting dinner for company, we never have to stop and run to the basement, because the pressure is way down. There is very little expense involved with our water system, just an occasional change of leather and that requires no mechanical ability. As for hot water, we have our old reliable teakettle. For heating wash water we use the iron kettle and feel it is a luxury because in many parts of the world the people do their laundry in the creeks.

Heating? We have no central heating system, not even an enameled stove. All we have is the same black model which for many is only a childhood memory. When coming inside, how comfortable to warm our chilling fingers. Where else could we toast our feet so satisfactorily and feel the warmth seep upward through the veins? Of course it must be fed and in zero or sub-zero temperatures, it's a starving creature. But with the basement filled with wood, which the members of our family have labored so generously to provide for us, what more could we ask? When I look at the ricks of wood, I feel humbly grateful for I know that in the world, many people are cold, living in huts, without even a blanket.

We have no padded or overstuffed seats to sit down upon. All we have are the lightweight hickory rockers and they are so portable. If we need more light we carry one to the window, if we're cold we carry it to the stove and prop up our feet in a very un-lady-like manner on the nickel trimmings of our stove. If someone comes with a baby, the rocker can be moved to the bedroom for there it is quiet. When it comes to entertainment we have the very best. Mother Nature is our Master Performer—the beauty of bare branches etched in front of a colorful sunset. I wonder how many people ever notice the varying branch formations on different trees. The cool colors of a winter sunrise are often overlooked by sleepy eyes. The ever-changing sky always has something interesting to see. The fluffy clouds of summer, the turbulence of a windy day in spring, or a heavy snowfall in winter, each season has its attractions.

In our leisure time we often watch our little feathered friends. It is a thrifty form of entertainment with a home-made bird feeder, homegrown sunflower and squash seeds and corn. How exciting to see our first evening grosbeak! The pileated woodpecker may be as homely as a mudpie but it is still a rare sight to behold. The saucy chickadee darts between the suet and feeder, almost faster than the eye can see. Even some kinds of our lowly sparrows are very attractive.

For real excitement on the farm, there's nothing like gathering in the first eggs from a flock of chickens you've raised from baby chicks. Nor is there anything as tasty as vegetables you've hoed and cultivated till you're hot and tired. When we stop to consider, it's nothing short of a miracle when we behold how much God provides for us to eat, all from one little dried-up dead-looking seed.

No, we have no so-called modern conveniences, but we are blessed with an abundance of life's necessities. We don't have an over-flowing grocery cart, or beautiful clothes or a big bank account to fall back on.

But I do have a family and friends, and many people I meet on life's highway. I have good eyesight, a healthy mind and body. I AM RICH.

> May I remember to be as rich with gratitude as I
> am rich with gifts which God has bestowed upon me.

Anonymous—Reprinted from *Family Life*

Much of the Amish educational process takes place at home. Amish parents feel that their children belong to them rather than to the state and that it is their obligation to educate them in the totality of the growing up process. All Amish adults are models in this educational process. However, the chief adult models of the Amish culture are the farmer and the housewife. The Amish religion is most compatible with farming and it is understood that children will some day farm or be a farmer's wife. Both boys and girls are given farming-related responsibilities around the ages of four and five. Four- and five-year-olds can be seen pumping water by hand and are also taught how to milk cows and do other farm related chores. Amish boys will be doing field work with horses by the time they are six or seven years old. I remember when six, my father put me on a two-horse, single-row, corn cultivator and I started down the corn row. I had not yet learned how to turn the horses around at the end of the field and head them back the other direction. Therefore, my older brother, just one corn row over with his horses, reached the end of the field at approximately the same time as I, turned my horses around and sent us back the other direction. This process continued until I learned to turn my team alone. Also, at a very young age I had certain cows assigned to me for milking both night and morning. Our 20 plus cows all had Amish-type names and the ones assigned to me at that age were gentle ones.

An Amish child learns early in life that work is a moral directive. Amish people generally rise around 4:30 or 5:00 in the morning. The lanterns are lit and they go to the barn to milk the cows and do the other farm-related activities. It is true that Amish youngsters work hard, but in actuality, pleasure becomes associated with work.

People often ask about the Amish parental method of teaching their children about sex. Actually, there is very little teaching by the parents. Yet, in my opinion, the Amish may have one of the more healthy outlooks regarding sex of any cultural group known. Perhaps some things are better left not said than to be communicated in a confusing and insincere manner. However, although not necessarily encouraged to do so, Amish children observe the sexual acts of farm animals and are often present at animal births. Their notions and emotions, regarding sex, are not contaminated by television, movies and otherwise as is often the case in the turbulent culture that surrounds these children. An Amish male has an eye for female beauty; however, her beauty is not camouflaged by make-up and perfume, and her weight is not a factor. The Amish youths' feelings regarding sex spring naturally from their surroundings. And, sexual deviates and perverts are unknown to Amish communities. I have no knowledge of an Amish homosexual or "gay" and have never heard the term, or its equivalent, used by an Amish person to describe another Amish individual's sexual preference.

It is evident from the essays and letters appearing in this section that the Amish are truly a hardworking, peace-loving sect. They are very humble people and children are taught this value early in life. And, the home, the church and the school all teach the same values. Amish youngsters are taught to fill their places in the little community as it has been planned for them; they are not taught individuality nor how to make their place in the "world." They are taught the values of honesty, thrift, love and purity. These values, lived by Amish adults, gain their children's allegiance. And, Amish children are not exposed to books, television shows nor movies that teach opposing values. Thus, they live what they learn and learn what they live.

Some social scientists have long stated that mankind has an innate, violent and aggressive nature. The more than 100,000 Old Order Amish people contradict this. Humility, as well as violence (like strapping big guns on little boys, my dad used to say), can be taught, according to the Amish parents.

There is a good deal of evidence to suggest that the Amish maintain what is perhaps the strongest and most stable family system in America. Their family patterns are not different from those of the other cultural institutions within their society. The Amish parents fortify their children with habits of understanding and generosity which enable them to make adequate adjustments to other segments of their society.

Section III

Rules for Living

The Orders of the Church

Throughout this book reference has been made to specific details that may not be applicable to all Old Order Amish church districts. Each district has its own unique *Ordnung* or Church Orders. For example, there was a small Orange County, Indiana Amish settlement where males began their beards when baptized into the church. However, as mentioned previously, in my former community none of the six church districts require the male to grow a beard until marriage. It should be acknowledged that this Orange County Amish group ran into extreme difficulties with the Indiana law requiring the orange, slow moving vehicle (SMV) emblem to be affixed to their buggies. Several were jailed for refusing to affix the sign to their buggies. Finally, in the mid-seventies, the entire community emigrated to South America in search of religious freedom. (This will be discussed in detail in Section VI.)

Church districts within each Amish community are formed geographically in such a manner so as to consist of around 50 families each. An Amish family may cross districts to attend church, especially if services of another district are being held in a close relative's home. However, if a family attends another district's service, they must abide, if at all possible, by that church's *Ordnung* for that particular Sunday.

Amish church *Ordnung* are almost never put into writing. Recently, I wrote several Amish ministers requesting copies of their church's *Ordnung* and had several responses indicating that none existed (in writing) for their church. Thus, I was surprised to receive the following from an Old Order Amish minister from a midwestern state. He wrote in part, **"This is close to what we follow here in _____, but we don't give copies to the members. Please** *don't use my* **name or district."**

I think the reader will agree that it would take a lot of self-discipline and a true belief in God to follow such firm and strict "orders" in the nineteen-nineties!

Church Ordinances

No ornamental, bright, showy form-fitting, immodest or silk-like clothing of any kind. Colors such as bright red, orange, yellow and pink not allowed. Amish form of clothing to be followed as a general rule. Costly Sunday clothes to be discouraged. Dresses not shorter than halfway between knees and floor, nor over eight inches from floor. Longer advisable. Clothing in every way modest, serviceable and as simple as scripturally possible. Only outside pockets allowed on work *oberhem* **(pants) or** *voma* **(coat) and pockets on large overcoats. Dress shoes, if any, to be plain and black only. No high heels and pomp slippers. Dress socks, if any, to be black except white for foot hygiene for both sexes. A plain, unshowy suspender without buckles (males of all ages must wear suspenders).**

Hat to be black with no less than 3-inch brim and not extremely high in crown. No stylish impressions in any hat. No pressed trousers. No sweaters.

Prayer covering to be simple, and made to fit head. Should cover all the hair as nearly as possible and is to be worn wherever possible. Pleating of caps to be discouraged. No silk ribbons.

Young children to dress according to the Word as well as parents. No pink or fancy baby blankets or caps.

Women to wear shawls, bonnets and capes in public. Aprons to be worn at all times. No adorning of hair among either sex such as parting of hair among men and curling or waving among women.

A full beard should be worn among men and boys before baptism if possible. No shingled hair. Length at least halfway below top of ears.

No decorations of any kind in buildings inside or out. No fancy yard fences. Linoleum, oilcloth, shelf and wall paper to be plain and unshowy. Overstuffed furniture or any luxury items forbidden. No doilies or napkins. No large mirrors, fancy glassware, statues or wall pictures for decorations.

No embroidery work of any kind. Curtains either dark green rollers or black cloth. No boughten dolls.

No bottle gas or high line electrical appliances.

Stoves should be black if bought new.

Weddings should be simple and without decorations. Names not attached to gifts.

No ornaments on buggies or harness.

Tractors to be used only for such things that can hardly be done with horses. Only either stationary engines or tractors with steel tires allowed. No air-filled rubber tires.

Farming and related occupations to be encouraged. Working in cities or factories not permissible. Boys and girls working out away from home for world people forbidden except in emergencies.

Worldly amusements as radios, card playing, party games, movies, fairs, etc. forbidden. Reading, singing, *Bible* games, relief work, giving of tithes, etc. are encouraged.

Musical instruments or different voice singing not permissible. No dirty, silly talking or sex teasing of children.

Usury (interest) forbidden in most instances. No government benefit payments or partnership in harmful associations. No insurance. No photographs.

No buying or selling of anything on Sunday. It should be kept according to the principles of the Sabbath. Worship of some kind every Sunday.

Women should spend time in doing good or reading God's Word instead of taking care of canaries, goldfish or house flowers.

Church confession is to be made if practical where transgression was made. If not, a written request of forgiveness should be made to said church. All manifest sins to be openly confessed before church before being allowed to commune. I Tim. 5:20. A period of time required before taking new members into full fellowship.

Because of a great falling away from sound doctrine, we do not care to fellowship, that is hold communion, with any churches that allow or uphold any unfruitful works of darkness such as worldliness, fashionable attire, bed-courtship, habitual smoking or drinking, old wives fables, non-assurance of salvation, anti-missionary zeal or anything contrary to sound doctrine.

Ordnung Reasons

Because the *Bible* does not specify a certain mode of dress, some people seem to think the church does not have the right to say what we should wear. But let us not forget that neither does the word of God in a specific way say that infant baptism is wrong, yet our forefathers were willing to give their lives rather than practice it. Neither is specific mention made of gambling, movies, radios, bed-courtship, etc., yet we believe they are wrong.

Webster's definition of luxury is the free indulgence in food and liquor, dress or equipage. Living in luxury is condemned. Having costly modern machinery, furniture, an auto, electricity, etc. would also come into that class.

To have all these things a person usually has to invest much money that might well be used otherwise. It can also cause people to go into debt deeper. Those with tractors usually farm more land, sometimes taking it away from poor people.

Following certain rules regarding suspenders, window curtains, clothing, etc. does not mean that any church having any different rules regarding these items is necessarily wrong. We believe it is the right and the duty of our church to observe any restrictions that would help to keep its members from being tempted so much to buy or wear fashionable clothes or to be found in places of worldly amusements, etc.

Take, for example, window curtains. We have no doubt that the two kinds mentioned are sufficient and also scriptural and do not give an appearance of decorations. But that is not saying that churches having other curtains are wrong provided they are plain. But any lace, fancy or showy curtain is wrong anywhere.

As to buckle suspenders, we do not believe they violate any scripture if they can be had strictly plain. But as plain ones are oftimes hard to get and oftimes those that are bought are not plain, we believe it would be better to use the others.

From what the old testament says about the beard...it is evident that it was considered a shame for a man to be without a beard and that full beard was worn. And why should we now be ashamed to look as God created us if He created us in His image? ...So if we change the image in which we were created, doesn't it look as if we were not satisfied with the way God created us?

As to the length of hair, if we stop to look how we are created, hair on the head grows out profusely perhaps a little over halfway below the top of the ears. We have scripture that we shall not wear them long like woman, therefore it appears the above length would be having them as God intended.... Furthermore, there are not two sets of rules given for members of the church, so if it is necessary to wear a beard upon marriage, it is also necessary on baptism.

Jesus said the world hates Him because He testifies that its works are evil. Therefore if we testify that it is wrong to do unnecessary work on Sunday as we believe it is to pick up milk and take care of it on Sunday, and at the same time would be a cause of them picking it up and taking care of it, would this be consistent?

The foregoing ordinances are considered the nearest scriptural under present day conditions, but should not be considered unchangeable, as different circumstances may require different regulations.

There could much more be written but to explain everything in detail would require several books. We hope everyone who reads this will be willing to live up to the enlightenment he has and also realize that no person or church is perfect for our knowledge is only in part.

Therefore should anyone find anything they consider unscriptural, we hope they will show Christian charity towards us and not remain silent. We hope, with God's help, to be ready to be admonished at any time, if in harmony with the Word.

Personal correspondence

Writer wishes to remain anonymous

Footwashing

The Amish are one of the few remaining sects, if not the only one, who still practice footwashing. This occurs during communion services twice each year. When the bishop indicates that it is time for this part of the communion service, the deacons and helpers carry in several buckets of lukewarm water and the foot washing begins. The sexes remain separate in this activity. When a same-sex pair completes this activity, they kiss one another on the cheek and "give alms" (money) to the poor. The church orders in several Amish communities require one person washing another person's feet to remain in a "stooped" position. However, in my community, one is permitted to kneel. This may seem trivial to the reader, but not to the Amish. If your church orders indicate that the washer should remain "stooped" so be it! To do otherwise would be viewed as breaking church orders and would not be tolerated. As the following Amish persons writes, which position to use is taken very seriously.

Amish church members, those who have been baptized (and are in good standing) practice footwashing twice a year. The church orders in several Amish communities require the person washing the other person's feet to remain in a "stooped" position. However, in my former community, one is permitted to kneel.

The Most Humble Position?

I am wondering what others think on the subject of feet washing. Is there one acceptable way to wash the other brother or sister's feet? Some people think you must bend over your back with straight knees so as to be in subjection to the other person.

It seems to me, if there ever was a time that it should be left up to the individual person as to what seems to him the proper position to do something, it should be in this. When a woman bends over (even if she has on a long dress) her dress goes up. I feel kneeling can be just as lowly as then your whole body is brought low. All through the *Bible* we read that God looketh on the heart, and not on the outward appearance of things. Who is qualified to tell the other man what is the lowliest or most humble way?

Anonymous—Reprinted from *Family Life*

Symbolism of Dress

It is difficult to distinguish that which is and is not religion in the Amish community. Religion is a seven-day-a-week affair, and everything one does and, especially the manner in which one dresses, is based upon religion. When one Amish person sees another, the clothing is recognized as having religious significance.

An Amish woman's hair is never cut and they are not seen publicly with their hair hanging loosely. My own stepmother's hair hung well below her waist. However, only members of her family ever saw her with her hair unbraided. I can only remember a few rare occasions. And, she always had her head covered, usually with the prayer veiling.

The women's prayer veiling or head covering is extremely important in Amish dress. A woman seen without her veiling on her head is considered a sinner. My stepmother even wore her covering to bed with the explanation that she may awaken at night and wish to pray. A young Amish girl writes:

My Covering

The *Bible* says that it is a shame for a girl to have her head uncovered and I think even little girls should wear it to school.

Mom says the covering should cover half your ears and always be tied under your chin. I always wear mine to school....

Esther, fourth grade

Although Amish people would be the last to say that their clothes will take them to heaven, they do believe, as does the Amish lady who wrote the following letter to the *Family Life*, that their clothing is often a protection against "**worldly**" influences and dangers.

The Power of the Covering

I appreciated the article on the covering. Although I have known it is an ordinance of God, yet the article did help to clarify the point for me.

It reminded me of an incident which happened some time ago. My daughter and I were waiting at a bus depot and decided to walk around the block to pass the time. We saw a bookstore across the street as we wanted to see whether they had anything of interest.

As we started down the small flight of stairs, one of the men came outside to meet us. "I'm very sorry," he said, "but women aren't allowed in here."

He seemed to be very courteous and friendly and visited with us awhile, asking whether we are from Pennsylvania, and so forth.

Of course I was greatly surprised to be turned away from a bookstore, but after a hasty glance into the show window I knew the reason and was glad to leave.

It seems strange that someone who will put pornographic literature on display for the public can feel shame to have his merchandise seen by someone he takes for a Christian. His actions showed that he knew better than he was doing.

I feel that we have at times been protected from annoyance, humiliation or worse because of our covering and plain clothes. Only God knows, yet there are so many people who are ashamed to wear them.

Anonymous—Reprinted from *Family Life*

Amish people always speak of dressing modestly. To dress modestly, especially for a female, is to have only the skin of her hands and face uncovered. Also, dressing modestly means wearing loose-fitting dresses, covered entirely with a loose-fitting cape so, as the following teenager writes, **"not to show body form and attract the opposite sex to self."**

Wearing Capes

If mothers expect their daughters to realize why they have to wear the cape dress, then the mothers will have to do their part first. They must see to it that their little girls wear aprons on their dresses in their young years. If Mother doesn't make the apron and prefers to have her little dresses done up in trimmings or puffed out, how can she expect her girls to wear the cape dress when they are grown? She must teach the meaning to it. These things start when the children are small. If

Mother changes patterns it will be planted in the children to do likewise. She must teach the meaning, too. First, so as to be separate from the world. Second, so to be modest, not to show body form and attract the opposite sex to self.

Anonymous—Reprinted from *Family Life*

The Amish people also dress modestly to be "**chaste, decent and unpretentious**" and to help boys "**keep their thoughts and actions pure from fleshly lusts.**"

More than Tradition

It has long been the practice among our plain churches for the women to wear a cape. But the reason for wearing it is being questioned, and I have even heard of mothers who could not explain why we wear a cape. Some think the cape is an unnecessary article, a hangover of tradition. But let's not miss the point so far. What we do should be scriptural. In I Timothy 2:9 we read, "...that women adorn themselves in modest apparel...."

Now the word modest is defined as chaste, decent and unpretentious. Unpretentious means not showy, or no unnecessary show. But without a cape (or with a fitted cape) we make an unnecessary show of our figure. Young girls may not realize what a struggle boys have to keep their thoughts and actions pure from "fleshly lusts" which I Peter 2:11 exhorts to abstain from. The whole *Bible* teaches that the lusts of the people corrupt a nation. We should learn to help each other. If we sisters by our immodest dress hinder others from thinking pure and holy thoughts we are helping them go the wrong direction.

Anonymous—Reprinted from *Family Life*

Amish people realize their dress is peculiar to the outside world. And, like the young Amish lady who wrote the following, they may have thoughts of dressing **"like the world,"** but, in the long run they're happy to dress differently.

It Does Make a Difference

It was a warm sticky summer evening when I went to a nearby shopping center to do some shopping. I was wearing what I thought was a long dress and I am ashamed to confess that there was a wee bit of envy and resentment in my heart when I saw the other girls and women in the store wearing cool shorts, halters and mini-skirts. Why do I always have to look so different and wear such clothing in this kind of weather, I thought? There is probably no one in this whole store that doesn't think I'd be smarter to dress a little cooler. It probably doesn't mean a thing to anybody in here that I dress this way except to think I'm dumb.

As I walked along, I heard a voice behind me, "Say, it sure is nice to see a young girl dressed decently," a man was talking and he was in earnest. "When you see all these women wearing barely anything, it almost makes you sick." With that he turned and walked away. I was left with a warm glow around my heart and a changed outlook. I decided that if it meant something to him, it probably does to a lot more people. No longer did I resent looking different for I was glad I could.

Anonymous—Reprinted from *Family Life*

As previously mentioned, Amish women believe they should never dress so as to "attract" a male. In the following short essay, a distressed Amish mother writes to an unknown Amish girl (or perhaps a Mennonite) who was dressed so as to cause **"a man to commit adultery in his heart,"** and to be **"responsible for sending boys to hell."**

To The Unknown Daughter

I don't know whose daughter you are, but you are one of God's creatures as well as I am, hence a sister whom I love. It has been several months since I saw you there in the hospital lobby. I never met you before or since, but your face keeps coming back to me. A pleasing face, not one to win a beauty contest perhaps, but one that anyone could love. Looking at your face, I would guess you come from a good family.

My grown son was with me and we were sitting on a seat across from where you sat. I wanted to talk to you, but I am the bashful kind, not apt to start a conversation with strangers. Anyway, it's too late now, the opportunity is gone.

I can't forget the picture you made. When you walked in, your skirt was short and it wasn't tight at all. I think perhaps it might have been just as well if it had been tighter. You swung your leg up high, resting your calf on the knee of the opposite leg. It seems to me the devil himself could not devise a better way to make a man commit adultery in his heart, which is enough to keep him out of heaven.

While you sat there, I suffered intensely. I know now I should have spoken to you, even with all those people about, but I missed my chance.

Don't you have a mother? Or doesn't she care either if you are responsible for sending boys to hell where they will suffer forever (as well as yourself)? This is a strong statement but we cannot ignore the truth just because it is terrible to think about. I can't believe you didn't know how you looked. There are many others just like you in the world today and you must have seen for yourself already. Does that in any way make it better just because many others are doing it?

There you sat for a whole hour or more in a position inexcusable for anyone except a small child. What made it all the more agonizing was the fact that you

had a prayer covering on your head.

Anonymous— Reprinted from *Family Life.*

Very little is written in the Amish literature about the dress of the male. However, many articles and letters are written about the dress of the females. This is not to say that the dress of the Amish male is unimportant; it simply is seldom written or talked about. Of course, this could be due to the fact that Amish males do practically all of the writing and it is their Biblical duty to make certain that women and children remain within the *Ordnung.*

Humility

Non-Amish writing about the Amish people almost always describe them as being a gentle, humble people. To an Amish person, humility is a virtue and pride is a cardinal sin. Often Amish homes are even without mirrors.

I have, on several occasions, been to Amish school planning meetings where humbleness (it seemed to me) almost got in the way of accomplishing that for which we were meeting. No one wants to speak first. When an Amish person speaks in their type meetings, they apologize for what they say and for speaking too long regardless of how long they spoke! An Old Order Amish writer indicates, in the following article, just how difficult it is to be genuinely humble in today's world.

My Struggle Against Pride

I felt pretty good about our buggy. We had given it a new coat of paint, which it had needed badly, and also made some other improvements. Being human, pride wanted to come into my heart. I wondered if other people would notice our shiny buggy, and whether they would comment on it. I tried to steer away from such thoughts, and concentrate on the real reason why we go to church. Certainly it wasn't to show off our buggy!

Satan persisted and as we were on our way to church, I was still struggling against vain thoughts. Then we passed a parked car with the words and a symbol meaning, "I love Jesus." Suddenly I felt humbled. Here I, a professing Christian, was on my way to church with my heart filled with pride, while on a "worldly" person's car was a simple meaningful expression of love to Jesus.

I cannot honestly say that Satan left me immediately, but those words gave me food for thought, and I again prayed for strength to overcome the evil within me.

Although I do not feel we should go around with bumper stickers on our buggies, I felt thankful to God that He helped me see those words at a time I needed them. Wouldn't it be good if we could carry this symbol of love to Jesus in our hearts at all time, and let it shine forth to others? Then they could see that we love Jesus.

Anonymous—Reprinted from *Family Life*

Nicknaming

Although nicknaming is common among the Amish, it is generally unknown to outsiders. The nicknames may originate from any event imaginable and will usually remain with the family down through generations. Nicknaming occurs because so many Amish have identical first and last names and this appears the only way to differentiate among themselves. Amish history indicates that there are less than fifty different last names among the over 100,000 Old Order horse and buggy Amish in America. Thus, nicknaming is an absolute necessity. Our family is known as "Dixie." The grapevine said this was because my grandfather purchased a farm from an outsider family named "Dixie." And David, my father's brother, was known as David "Dixie." But complications arise when brothers have sons and give them, as they frequently do, the same Biblically inspired first name. This results in one of the two (usually both) getting a first name nickname also.

An Amish person, however, never calls another Amish individual by one's nickname to one's face. It is done only in conversations with others since it is most times used only to correctly identify someone in the quickest possible manner. However, sometimes nicknames are used when making a joke or a derogatory statement about someone. And, it is personally very embarrassing for one to be called by one's nickname. However, they know that others refer to them this way. It is traditional and a way to avoid confusion in a system where so many have the same name. Females never have a first name nickname. Aside from "Dixie" there is "Bottle," "Turkey," "Tag," "Hey-Hey," "Gander," "Fish," "Cream," "Banty," "Jack," "Codger," and many, many others in my former Amish community. The father's nickname always becomes the last name of the offspring. Of course, females take on their husband's nicknames, but for the male, it is his forever. Seldom do nicknames flatter anyone. They are usually comical in nature and may be viewed by the "owner" as derogatory and even demeaning.

Church Services and Ordaining Ministers

The Old Order Amish attend church services in a member's home every other Sunday with the Sunday between set aside for visiting purposes. On this Sunday Amish people visit the homes of the sick, the homes of new babies, relatives or friends.

Depending on the size, an Amish settlement is generally divided into six church districts. That is to say, there is a North church, a Northeast church, a Northwest church and so forth. Everyone knows the particular boundaries and "orders" (rules) for each church district and will generally attend services in their own district. However, this does not mean that a member of the North district, for example, cannot attend church in the Southwest district. As stated previously, crossing church boundaries is very common, especially if the services are held in a close relative's home who lives in a neighboring district. The rules generally remain similar across the church districts within a particular community. However, there may be small, but distinct differences from one district to another. For example, in my former community, the church district permitted rubber tires on the buggy while a neighboring district had the wheels rimmed in steel. One similarity across all church districts in all Amish communities is that religious services are conducted in German.

Each church district may have as many as eight ministers and all will speak during the service which normally beings at 8:30 a.m. Usually, the minister who closes the service around one o'clock p.m. will announce in whose home services will be held two weeks from that day.

It is a large responsibility to host the church services. This means a thorough cleaning of the house and the barn, and the fences are fixed and things are painted. If it is summertime, the trees will be whitewashed (with a lime/water solution which begins to fade with the first rain) about six feet up the trunk. Of course, the woman of the house will prepare a meal to be served to everyone following the services. Cookies are served to children during the service. No longer partaking of the cookies is an obvious sign of "maturity." Older children who do take cookies are teased by their peers. This church Sunday noon meal was a tradition in my community in that it consisted only of coffee, homemade bread, jams, peanut butter thinned with maple syrup, canned beets and pickles. In my sixteen years of attending Amish church services, I observed very little variation in this particular menu. And, to my knowledge, it has not changed today.

If it is a large Amish community, three church services will be conducted in three separate homes and one will host the young people for their Sunday evening sing. That is to say, the young folks (those sixteen and older but unmarried) of the entire community gather at only one of the homes where church services were conducted that day rather than in three. The woman whose house is chosen will also prepare a meal for the young folks that evening. This meal goes far beyond the menu offered at noon. Both the church services and the evening sings spill over into the barn, especially in the large Amish districts in Lancaster, Pennsylvania.

Another duty of the host family is to go to the home where the church services were held two weeks prior and obtain the hearse-like wagon filled with the backless benches used for all religious services within the district. These backless benches are generally made of oak, are very sturdy and varnished to perfection. The family hosting church services will have pushed the furniture into corners and the benches take up the entire house. Benches will be placed upstairs, in the basement, in the main part of the house, and if need be, in the barn. The sexes remain separate during all religious services. After the members are

---

seated (married men in the front of the preachers; young, un-married females are seated directly behind these men; married females and small children sit in the dining room and kitchen, and others are scattered throughout the house) the *vorsinger*, the one leading the singing, begins the first song. The *vorsinger* has the informal training required but does not sit or stand in any special place. His training comes from his observation and imitation throughout the years. As stated previously, the Amish songs are not set to music, are thus difficult to sing, and to the uninformed, the singing sounds like wailing or chanting. The *vorsinger* sings the beginning of each new line of a hymn alone. The *vorsinger* duty switches to a different man with each song. The second song of every Amish church service is always the *"Lob Lied"* during which the ministers retire for council. The congregation continues to sing while the preachers are in council, but cease immediately on their return. As soon as the services end, the men carry the benches outside and the women set up the large tables for the noon meal. Men and children always eat first.

The Amish do not use trained ministers. And, as Judas' replacement was made via the casting of lots, so are Amish ministers chosen. Thus, an Amish married male may go to church on a particular Sunday as a lay person and return home that evening a minister! He will receive no compensation for this very responsible and diligent work as a minister. And, he will continue to farm and do all duties expected of any married Amish male.

No Amish person ever openly expresses a desire to be a minister as this would indicate self-pride. The only way to become a preacher is to be "hit" by the "casting of the lot." On the Sunday the new minister is to be ordained, an existing minister takes nominations from the congregation. The nominations are whispered to the ministers. As many *Ausbunds* (song books) as there are nominees are placed on a bench in front of the congregation. Only one *Ausbund* has a note saying "You are the one" (written in German) also with particular *Bible* verses, in it. Extreme anxiety surrounds the casting of the lot and sadness prevails.

Sadness is a common feeling on the day ministers are chosen. One of my uncles used to talk about this concerning himself and he was once nominated for the lot. Later he told me that he was not really concerned about getting that "particular piece of paper" (making him a minister for life) because he had not been " called" by God. I remember being present at several of these services when ministers "were made" (as the Amish call it) and on each occasion the man chosen by the lot invariably indicated that he "just knew he would get the paper." Each had felt the "call" from God to serve.

The wife of an Amish minister has no definable role to play. She simply needs to be a good housekeeper, a good wife and a good Christian. Her life is difficult for she, like her husband, is a model for other Amish to follow. Of course, it is also difficult to be an offspring of an Amish minister as the following short essay implies.

Amish ministers have no formal training and are chosen by the "casting of the lot". That is, a married Amish male may attend services on a given Sunday morning as a lay person and return home that evening as a minister for life. There is no financial compensation and ministers are expected to lead an exemplary life worthy of emulation by all. Amish sermons are long, biblically explicit and detailed. However, no notes of any sort may be used by the minister. Thus, they must spend many long hours in preparation for their Sunday delivery.

A Minister's Daughter

Even though I had a decent set of friends. I was only human and sometimes wished to make my things a little more fancy than I should have. I have never forgotten what my dear mother told me one day when I asked why I couldn't sew a wider hem on my dress. She said, "I don't believe you'd want it if you knew how many of the other girls are watching you. Seeing you with fancy things, they will say, 'She's a minister's daughter, and if she may do that, I may, too.'" My mother went on to explain that she wasn't a minister's daughter, but she watched the minister's girls and sort of used them as an example. She also told me that often our actions will affect the sermons my dad preaches. His words lost a lot of strength if his children are not abiding by the rules of the church.

This was a lesson for me. I could not help it that I was the daughter of an ordained man, but I did not want to be the reason that others went astray, or that my father's sermons would lose their effectiveness because of my disobedience. I saw that in a sense we had an added responsibility.

Anonymous—Reprinted from *Family Life*

Taking Care of Older Persons

It is nice to grow old as an Amish person. They do not use nursing homes and the elderly are revered and viewed as being wise. It is the responsibility of the young to care for the elderly—a responsibility never taken lightly.

The Amish life may seem bleak to some outsiders, but there is nothing bleak about their retirement customs. In fact, they are way ahead of modern day society when it comes to finding retirement contentment.

When an Amish farmer and his wife reach 70 or thereabouts, it is customary for them to move to a separate section of their home, or to a small house nearby known as *Grossdawdy's* (Grandfather's) *House*. Then one of their sons (usually the youngest) and his family move into the main house and take over the farming responsibilities.

The retired parents thus remain in familiar surroundings and have their privacy, yet they are close to members of their family. Although retired, there are still plenty of light chores around the farm to keep the elders happily occupied, such as tending the animals, keeping the building and grounds in order and assisting in the care of their grandchildren.

Perhaps the most appealing aspect of Amish retirement is the close relationship that is maintained with the family group. Children are taught from the cradle to "honor thy father and mother," "to take care of your own" and they generally marry and settle down within a few miles of their parents.

The close and affectionate ties which the elders thus maintain with their families, plus their firm religious faith and the economic independence, breeds an enviable contentment from most outsiders, and, in my opinion, helps avoid many of the physical and psychological ills so prevalent among the elderly of the "outsider" culture in America.

No Insurance or Involvement with the State

A large facet of Amish noninvolvement with the state is their refusal to accept government money. They turn down old-age pensions, Social Security payments and farm subsidies as unearned income and not acceptable. During World War II, a number of Amish farmers signed their milk subsidy checks over to township trustees for road maintenance. In the early seventies, the state of Pennsylvania passed a law providing state aid to parochial schools and the state authorities sent a $260,000 check to the Amish school officials. The check was returned to the state unendorsed! Many, many such examples could be given.

The Amish take care of their own. Twice a year money is collected for the widows and others who are unable to earn a living. Twice yearly offerings are the only time the plate is passed in church.

Instead of buying insurance policies, the Amish have their own system of mutual aid. If a barn burns down or cattle are struck by lightning, an appraisal is made by two or three Amish males and two-thirds of the cost is paid by the church. Members are assessed according to their tax duplicates. If the amount is too large for one congregation to absorb, it is spread over several districts.

A barn raising, particularly if it is to replace a burned building, is a great social occasion. People come from miles around to help. The men raise the huge precut beams (done by Amish craftsmen who are known as excellent carpenters) into place and the women prepare food. Oftentimes a structure is raised, roofed and covered with sideboards in a day. With hospital and medical costs rising, the Amish are facing the insurance dilemma. Some communities have gone to something known as the "Amish Aid Plan." However, the plan is controversial and is viewed as "insurance" by many Amish church groups and is thus rejected.

Holidays and Ceremonies

The Amish observe several special days as holidays. Among these are: Christmas, Good Friday, Easter, Ascension Day, Pentecost and Thanksgiving. Of course, weddings, which usually occur on Tuesday or Thursday (not during the harvest season), provide extra holidays. Barn-raisings, corn frolics and so forth also provide a type of "working" holiday for old and young alike.

Christmas was not very special at my house. And, I believe we were typical. I was never taught to believe in Santa Claus or anything even remotely similar. And, we certainly did not "cut down a young tree and foolishly bring it into the house like outsiders do" (as my father used to say) and we did not exchange presents. Each Christmas eve we children would find the largest plate available in our kitchen and set it at our individual place on the dining room table (your place at the table remains your place until you leave home) knowing that our dad would fill it with "goodies" sometime during the night. The "goodies" usually included homemade candy, nuts and caramel popcorn balls. And, on some very special times the plate may have a small package of "boughten potato chips" and "store bought candy bars."

The three holidays that I most vividly remember are Good Friday and the day proceeding both the Fall and Spring Church Communion. I did not like them because they were "fasting" days, so very unusual among the Amish who are good cooks and love to eat!

Health and Medicine

The Amish are not opposed to physicians or scientific medicine. However, they seldom seek the advice of an MD for colds and so forth and they favor quasi-medical cures. The advice of the doctor is seldom sought until other remedies have been tried. I could document several cases of Amish people dying from what they thought was a minor ailment before seeking the advice of the "outsider" physician.

Illness becomes major news in the Amish community and is a topic of interest in the *Budget* (the Amish weekly newspaper). The length of a person's illness is often measured by how many church meetings that person misses. Sick persons are pampered by the community and friends and relatives spend much time visiting them.

Seldom do Amish women have their children delivered by an MD. This is still common today, but more and more Amish mothers are giving birth in local hospitals.

Although not opposed to surgery, dental work and anesthesia, they are often opposed to immunization. I well remember the hassel in my community when the public school authorities tried to enforce small pox immunization on the Amish. However, the authorities finally "winked" at the issue. Personally, I did not receive my Small Pox immunization until 1983 when preparing for a journey to India.

Although there are no Amish MDs, there is often an Amish person in the community who is called on to administer to the sick. This person does *Brauching*.

Sympathy-healing or *Brauching* played a role in my own Amish family. The German word *Brauch* is freely translated as "powwowing" and my grandmother was a "powwower." I was present on two occasions when she practiced her skill. Both times she moved a small shovel of red hot coals in circular motions around the "patient" and silently repeated verses and charms. Her lips moved vigorously but no words were ever uttered aloud. All the verses, charms and formulas are kept secret by the "powwower" and can only be passed along to a member of the opposite sex. Before grandmother died, in her early nineties, she passed her *Brauch* secrets along to my father (or at least I think so) who never once practiced the art. Late in his life he informed me that he simply did not believe in it. At no time was my grandmother looked upon as peculiar by other Amish people. However, we children were told not to discuss "powwowing" with "outsider" children at school as "they wouldn't understand." Such practices are still very prevalent among the Amish. However, most term the practice as "Faith Healing."

The *"brauch"* practice is currently a topic of controversy among the Amish. The following letters appearing in the December, 1989 edition of *Family Life* indicate that many now question the practice.

Faith Healing

...This practice is not dangerous because it is useless, but because it is deceptive—as the one seeking help will believe the answer is from God. People who use this practice tend to become addicted, or continually need help the same as with drugs, bringing them into bondage. Where these practices are openly accepted, many questionable things will follow, as you mention. These will not build true faith and respect in our young people....

Anonymous—Reprinted from *Family Life*

And, a minister writes:

...I'm afraid of this. Even unbelievers can do these things. By far the most conditions that people *brauch* for will correct themselves without it. Our children were able to grow up without this, even though we live next to a good neighbor who does it for various ailments. In I Timothy 4:7 Paul admonishes Timothy, "But refuse profane and old wives' fables, and exercise thyself rather unto godliness."

I believe the young folks problems can almost certainly be traced to a lack of spiritual concern on the parents' part. However, to change longstanding ungodliness, we must work together and with the church. To me that is an important part of our repentance. This cannot be brought about by placing our faith in signs and superstitions. I believe *brauching* is well meant by most who practice it, but for my part I would feel more comfortable without it.

Anonymous—Reprinted from *Family Life*

Amish people will ride a bus or hire a "driver" and travel long distances to be "cured" of an illness. News of a "good doctor who can really cure" travels fast in an Amish community and this particular physician suddenly finds himself (they would not seek out a female physician) with several new Amish patients. Also, "doctor changing," much to the dislike of outsider physicians, is common among the Amish people.

Sadly, many Amish people are taken in by quacks. The *Budget* carries advertisements for all sorts of ointments and other type medicines that the Amish regularly purchase.

The Amish are constantly searching for home remedies and word travels fast when a new remedy is "discovered." It should be acknowledged that many of these home remedies do work and are often picked up and used by the "outsider" neighbors. Several years ago *Family Life* carried pleas from Old Order Amish people for home remedies for particular afflictions. The following are some answers to such pleas from the original *Home Remedy* section of *Family Life*.

For Colds

Boil one gallon dandelion flowers and one gallon hot water for five minutes. Let stand for three days. (It is best kept in a crock jug.) Strain. Then boil the peelings of two lemons and one orange with the dandelion water for 15 minutes. Let stand until luke-warm. Slice in the two lemons and the orange. Add two teaspoons yeast and three pounds of sugar and let stand for six days. Bottle.

For Athletes Foot

We experienced with an old remedy lately. It is also good for any infections such as swollen fingers around the nails or other sores from cuts or scratches.

Take one quart of wood ashes. Add one quart of water. Boil five minutes, stirring occasionally to keep from sticking to the bottom of pan. (Use stainless steel or enamelware. Never use aluminum. I use a basin, then I can just reheat it in the basin to use the next day.) When cooked five minutes add just enough water to cool, to soak your foot in (about two quarts). Have it as hot as you can stand it. Soak every evening ten minutes.

For Gallstones

With not much food in the stomach, the afflicted one should take a dose of ordinary olive oil at bedtime (six ounces). Take a little water with it to aid in swallowing. Then lie on right side to allow the oil to seep down into the gall bladder, which softens the stones, causing them to slip out easily. Take a small does of Epsom salts in the morning. The stones are easily identified, as they are green in color, and there will be anywhere from 20 to 200 of them. The gall bladder is not injured. Some victims have to oust them once a year.

For Warts

We have good results with castor oil. Soak a band-aid (gauze) and place over wart (*Pennsylvania*).

I put on castor oil and in time all disappeared. Our hired hand cleared his hands by washing them three times a day with baking soda. My brother-in-law healed his warts by rubbing them with raw potato peelings (*Indiana*).

For ordinary warts use the milky juice of the common dandelion—flower stem, leaf stem or root. Apply once or twice a day until the wart disappears (*Ontario*).

Rub each day with a piece of white chalk (*Indiana*).

Cut milkweed to get the milky juice. Put on several times (*Ohio*).

The tip of my forefinger was covered with warts for about six or seven years. Some grew under the nail so that the nail was pushed up, which bothered me at times. This spring when I planted garden, I used wood ashes in the rows where I planted carrots and radishes to help control root maggots. A few days afterwards the warts became sore and started to get smaller. In several weeks they were all gone except one. I put a bit of ashes on it, and it soon disappeared. *Ohio*

Anonymous—All from *Family Life*

Practicing the Common Courtesies

As mentioned previously, the Amish parents do not always teach their children that which the outsider terms "common courtesies." *Family Life* carried several essays, both pro and con, concerning the notion of knocking on a neighbor's door before entering. The following essay best explains their reasons for not knocking.

Door Knocking

...It is a challenge for each of us to try to regulate the affairs of our household so that if anyone were to step inside the front door unannounced we would not need to be ashamed. It is an unwritten law that among our people we do not take baths, or appear half-dressed, inside the front door. We have private rooms where we go to take care of our private needs and it is well that it is so. I would like to relate an incident which happened a number of years ago to illustrate this point.

Early one morning a man went to his neighbor's house to make arrangements for the day's work. As he stepped inside the door, the family, and it was a large family, was at the breakfast table. His entrance took them a bit by surprise, and before he had time to see what was going on, one of the girls quickly rose from the table and made a hasty departure to the upstairs of the house. The truth was that she was not dressed as was fitting for anyone to be at the breakfast table. That was the reason for her sudden departure.

Who was at fault? Was it the unexpected visitor, or was it the girl who insisted on coming to the breakfast table in such a state as not to be presentable to the neighbor? I am afraid it was the latter, and if we are to maintain the simplicity of our way of life, then we will have to keep up our standards that we are ready to welcome our brother at any time of the day at least inside of the front door.

Most of our houses are built so we can see the lane from the kitchen table. Where this is not the case, then it would be especially wise to announce our coming in some way such as slamming a door in going through the summer kitchen or in some other way. If we open the main door slowly, it immediately signifies that someone else except a member of the family is there (Who ever heard of a member of the family opening the door slowly?) Once inside the door, if no one is present, we can listen if perhaps the family is engaged in family devotions or other matters which would be private. If this is not the case then we can always say "Hello" or some other word of greeting which will announce our presence in a way that should not be embarrassing.

Looking in the *Bible*, we cannot find anything definite on the matter.

When Peter escaped from prison he knocked at the door where the church was assembled (Acts. 12:13). But this really does not prove anything because due to obvious reasons the door was locked and this was the only way in which he could make his presence known. We would hardly believe, that he would have taken the time to knock if the door would have been unbarred.

Anonymous—Reprinted from *Family Life*

Avenues of Communication

Many Amish do not subscribe to "worldly" newspapers or publications, as the *Budget* is the weekly newspaper for the Amish people. Scribes, one or two from each Amish community, write the news of their particular community to the *Budget* offices in Sugarcreek, Ohio. The editor is an outsider. Some examples:

Recent news from Berne was that, ""Jacob _____ was in a hospital."

Wrote the scribe from there: " one lung had filled up."

Elsewhere in the news, the scribe from _____ County reported without comment that "John Yoders spend Sunday at Joe Yutzy's to remind him of his 40th birthday."

And from Topeka, Indiana came word that a "little dishwasher came to stay at Amos _____ since 18th Dec..., named 'Rebecca.'"

To the average reader of today's newspapers, the above items might seem trivial and quaint. However, for the Amish people this news is of utmost importance. For them, the world is chronicled in eight gray columns covering 10 to 16 pages of a weekly newspaper.

The paper is unique in other respects. It has no staff writers, editorials, crossword puzzles or comic strips. Its strength, style and tone are derived from the "letters" from several hundred unpaid correspondents from around the world.

They report with simplicity, "a three-inch snowfall in Montgomery, Indiana" or that somebody "innocently walked off with the wrong shawl at Ann _____ funeral."

For many Amish the *Budget* is the only newspaper to enter their home. However, many now subscribe to the three Amish magazines published by Amish people in Alymer, Ontario. The three are: *Family Life, Blackboard Bulletin* and *Young Life.*

Family Life contains Views and Values, letters to the editor, World Wide Window, Staff Notes, Learning About Your Health, a Children's Section and stories relating to the Amish heritage, among many others. Its founding date was 1967.

The Blackboard Bulletin replaced the "circle letter" among Amish school teachers. A monthly publication, it focuses mainly on problems relating to Amish education. Each issue contains several teaching tips, written by Amish teachers, along with several essays written by Amish school children.

Young Life is written for young Amish adults and focuses on courtship practices and other aspects relating to Amish youth. Much is currently being written concerning the problem Amish youth are having in maintaining their values and customs.

Many more Amish rules for living could be written. However, the basic rules and regulations governing the lives of the Amish have been covered in this section.

Section IV

Courtship, Marriage and Death

Amish courting begins at age sixteen in most Amish communities and is known as *rum springa* or "running around." This age limit is strictly enforced by the other unmarried young people who are sixteen and beyond. Should a young man (in my former community) attend one of the Sunday evening Amish sings before his sixteenth birthday, he is teased and forcibly fed warm milk from a spoon. This playful ritual indicates to the young man that he is not yet mature enough to attend the "sings" and to date. Females not yet sixteen simply do not attend the Sunday evening sings (called "crowds"). This would reveal a rebellious nature that would not be tolerated.

Most everyone knows the exact day of a youth's sixteenth birthday and young men often look forward to a particular pretty young maiden's sixteenth birthday—it is a rite of passage! It is obvious that young Amish males and females yearn for their sixteenth birthday. In my former Amish community, age sixteen is viewed as a time of reaching adulthood—legislated maturity by the community. Upon reaching your sixteenth birthday, the Sunday afternoon becomes yours and you no longer are obligated to go home with your parents following church services to do the Sunday evening chores. To be given a Sunday evening free of farm-related chores is envied by one's younger siblings. In addition, a male is usually presented a horse and buggy as his own for his sixteenth birthday. In some communities, women are required to wear a loose fitting cape-like apron over their dress in keeping with their concept of modesty.

As mentioned in a previous section, church services are held in several homes simultaneously if the size of the Amish community so warrants. However, the youth singing, or "crowd" as termed in most communities, will generally be held in only *one* home that Sunday evening. The location of the singing is often a mystery. Yet, somehow, the youth from all the different church districts within that respective community seem to learn the location of the "crowd" and shortly after the "old-folks" leave the church services, the young folks begin to appear from throughout the community. A large meal is served to all by the host and hostess. The custom of keeping the sexes segregated during the church services also applies at the Sunday evening singing. For several hours or so the youth will sing and hold conversations. Of course, as in any group, not all the Amish youth will be inside the house singing. The Amish have their share of both males and females who break the rules and are sometimes seen as trouble-makers by the adults. Some of these "trouble-makers" may even bring home-brew to the "crowd," or may even have purchased beer or whiskey for the occasion. The only married people at the singing will be the owners of the particular farm where the youth are gathered. However, if the father of the household permits this forbidden type of activity to occur, he faces the wrath of the ministers and parents. Thus, many an Amish farmer has attempted to run the young, deviant trouble-makers from his farm. As can be imagined, most of the youth cannot get into the house and much of the singing and games occur in the barn and other locations. In the absence of modern lighting, exactly what goes on outside the house is sometimes difficult to control.

It is a well-known fact that Amish parents are lenient (it is almost a casual look-the-other-way attitude by some) with their sons who are between the age of sixteen and marriage. And, some young men (those who stay outside rather than go into the house to sing, for example) go on a "binge" or go "wild." It should be acknowledged that the term "wild" has different connotations for different cultures, i.e. (as stated in the following essay) making wise cracks and telling jokes are signs of being "wild" to the Amish adults. However, Amish adults nag these types of boys to "settle down." Two Amish adults write about this "**wild**" stage in the following letters to *Family Life*.

Our Children Need Their Parents

Something is wrong in our Christian churches but where is the root of the trouble? Children are running after the pleasures of this world. They smoke, drink, make wisecracks, run with the *wild* bunch, have smaller and smaller coverings and shorter dresses. They hide things they're not supposed to have so the parents don't find out. Why are they different from what Christian young folks used to be? Are they afraid of being looked down upon? Why do they come home and bring us the faults of others to try to cover up their own? Why do we as parents repeat these things to others behind their backs? Is it because of a lack of true Christian principles?

Have we taught our children to love their neighbors and not gossip about them or relate their faults to others? Or do we as parents still do these things? If we do, there is no wonder our children are doing them.

Anonymous—Reprinted from *Family Life*

Settling Down

It's a dangerous thing to pressure someone into "settling down" without insisting that he also "settle up." For it is quite possible for a young person to decide, when he gets tired of being nagged by the church and parents, that okay, he'll conform. He may be ready to get married anyhow, and stay at home. So he agrees to drop his "wild life," whatever that may include in his particular community. And relatives and parents, looking only on the outside, draw a sigh of relief—too soon. Far too often such a person has not really experienced an inner change. He has not really given himself up, surrendered and dedicated his life to God. What he does is not out of conviction. There is not depth to his spiritual life. He does not think to go aside for personal prayer. He does not cherish a tender conscience and a daily walk with God. The Bible doesn't interest him.

Thus the sowing-wild-oats-and-settling-down-later pattern becomes expected of young people—it is almost a family tradition, and the parents may become alarmed if their children don't follow it than if they do. But, no matter how accepted such reasoning and behavior has become in some communities, it is unscriptural. It is a blight on the church. It is unfair to young people, who often find out to their sorrow that they must reap what they have sown. We need to awaken to the spiritual harm this type of reasoning has done, and will continue to do unless it is stopped.

Reprinted from *Family Life*

The formal singing at the "crowd" generally concludes around 10:00 p.m. However, in most communities the young people do not pair off and go home at this hour. Rather, they play "ring" type games. These games are tolerated, but most adults (even though they may have taken part in them when young) question whether or not they are Christian activities.

The games are often played late into the night, however, couples usually begin to pair off around midnight. A young Amish man does not directly ask a girl for a date. He sends a "middle-man" to ask a particular girl to be his date following the "crowd." Even couples who are going steady will usually meet at a pre-arranged time or the young man will send a buddy to let his girlfriend know that he is now ready to take her home. Usually, especially if it is a first date, the young man will attempt to slip away from the singing without being noticed. If it is the first date, he will most certainly be followed to the young lady's home by a group of his Amish male and female friends. In my community, people who follow the young couple home are known as "cut-ups." They harass the young couple. They may remove the wheels from his buggy, turn his horse loose or do other types of mischievous deeds while he is attempting to court the young lady. The young lady's parents remain in the house and try to appear unconcerned. I remember one particular incident in which the "cut-ups" worked very hard taking a young man's buggy apart and rebuilt it straddle of the barn's roof peak—40 feet up!

Young men and women who have an interest in each other for dating purposes will seldom be seen together in daylight. Thus, a brother may bring his sister or a female cousin to the Sunday evening singing. These young people can be observed in any Amish community on a Sunday afternoon as they travel toward the singing in their open buggies. Should the buggy be overcrowded, the young men will be seated on the laps of the females. The reverse will not be observed. This is in keeping with the dominance of the male.

It is a commonly known fact that young Amish men spend a considerable amount of time at their date's home. Many a young Amish man has been seen traveling home in his buggy on a Monday morning as the sun is rising—sound asleep! However, when he does arrive home, he will receive no pity from his parents and will work the entire day. He will not get an opportunity to sleep until after the evening meal.

This practice of staying at his date's house till the wee hours of the morning may be the remnance of the courtship practice of bundling, which used to be prevalent in many Amish communities. There may still be Amish communities that practice bundling, or as it is often termed, "bed-courtship."

The practice of bundling has been defended by some Amish people on the basis that it was tradition, and tradition is sacred among the Amish. However, most Amish now condemn this practice. A recently married Amish female wrote the following letter to *Family Life* concerning her past bundling.

No More Bundling

I am thankful for the discipline my parents taught me, although at the time it all seemed so harsh, but now I feel it was not harsh enough. Since I'm married I've told them how glad I am that they made me dress plainly at all times and didn't allow me to go swimming, even though I cried then because I couldn't go. Now I have a sister who has just turned sixteen and already is going steady with a boy (whom I hold nothing against) but feel she is too young yet.

I told her if I could live that time of my life over again I wouldn't start dating until I'm at least eighteen. Nor would I practice bundling or go away that would require a stay overnight. Nor would I consider visiting with each other later than midnight necessary. All the talking, singing or reading can be done before this hour; longer visits only lead to other things which are not good.

Anonymous—Reprinted from *Family Life*

It is the writer's belief, based on the writing of Amish adults, that bundling will shortly be, if not already, a thing of the past for the Amish. It should be acknowledged that most Amish adults do not permit their children to bundle.

Because of uninformed non-Amish writers, many are led to believe that the Amish practice immoral courtship. However, this is simply not true. A letter was sent to *Young Companion* by a young Amish person seeking advice about what to do on a date. Some of the answers the person received in the next issue indicate that *most* Amish communities not only do not permit bed courtship but even discourage hand holding and especially **"kissing and hugging."**

Courtship

I may be wrong, but I am convinced most sincere young people conduct their courtship exactly in the way that is expected of them. The trouble is that their parents and the church do not expect enough. Nearly twenty years ago my wife and I were the first dating couple in a new Amish settlement where, I am thankful to say, high Christian standards were expected of us.

The church asked us to not see each other more often than once a week (less frequently at first); to be with each other no more than a few hours at a time; to always visit with each other in a well-lighted room. Hugging, kissing or petting were strictly out....

Anonymous—Reprinted from *Young Companion*

Premarital sex relations are disapproved of and condemned by the Amish elders and community. Transgressors are expelled from the church and shunned. However, reinstatement requires only a confession before the church assembly and a moral stigma does not remain with the couple.

There is a very low rate of illegitimate births among the Amish. It is common knowledge that in the case of an illegitimate pregnancy, marriage will follow. Rarely, if ever, is a great deal of pressure on the couple necessary. In rare cases when the identification of the father is questionable, an older man in the community, usually a widower, will marry the mother-to-be and raise the child as his own. If the child is born out of wedlock it is usually taken into the family by the girl's parents and, since marriage almost always follows shortly thereafter, the social or moral stigma is not lasting.

An Amish mother apologizes for the "**way we got married**" in the following letter to *Young Companion*.

...Yes, there a quite a few things I would do different if I could do them over again. The first thing is I would listen more to what my mother and father say. I would join church, not only because I had the age and everyone else did, but because I wanted to be born again. I'd want my husband and I to have a different courtship. How much better it would have been if we would not have kept such late hours. Maybe then we wouldn't have had a baby six months after we were married. We asked forgiveness before God and church, but we still have to reap what we sowed. We have to try and explain to our children to do as we say, not as we did.... I'm not sorry that I married who I did, and hope he feels the same way, too. But I'm sorry for the way we got married. So all you boys and girls, remember, what you sow that you must someday reap.

Anonymous—Reprinted from *Young Companion*

Because of the limited number of available marriage partners, there has always been a great deal of inbreeding among the Amish. Deleterious effects, such as a sixth finger or underdeveloped third breast in females are sometimes a direct result of inbreeding. Marriage between first cousins is now taboo and second cousin marriages, though frequent, are officially discouraged by the church. (This is discussed in more detail in Section VI.) However, to say the least, mate finding is sometimes difficult in a small Amish community where marrying "outside the faith" is strictly forbidden.

An Amish youth is permitted to marry a member of a more conservative church, but to marry someone from a more liberal Amish church group is forbidden. Because of scarcity of marriageable mates, it is becoming a common practice for a group of dating-age young people to spend a weekend visiting another Amish community. These groups visit one another usually via Greyhound buses and are known in the community as "strangers." The young people look forward to this group of "strangers." It is always a much talked-about occasion when word is received that a group of "strangers" from a distant Amish community will be visiting for the weekend.

There are basically only 50 or so different last names among the Amish. Thus, it is not at all uncommon for a young lady not to change her last name when she marries, i.e., Wittmers frequently marry Wittmers, Yoders marry Yoders and Bontragers marry Bontragers.

As mentioned previously, dating begins at age sixteen. However, the magic surrounding age sixteen is being questioned by both some young and older Amish. This questioning is evident in the following letters.

Dating Age

I think there is danger in dating too young, especially at sixteen. I myself started at seventeen and see now that it was bad because I was not serious about it and so dated many girls just for a good time. You might be serious at sixteen even if I wasn't, but I would still recommend waiting for a few years. By that time you would be able to consider marriage after dating for a suitable period.

Anonymous—Reprinted from *Young Companion*

I think parents should discourage sixteen and 17'ers from dating and going steady, instead of being proud of them when they do. Maybe if they would know everything, their proudness would turn to shame. Unless most sixteen and 17'ers are more mature than I was at that age it is best not to get serious about this, which is something that should not be anything but serious.

Anonymous—Reprinted from *Young Companion*

Some Amish communities have strict rules for determining the "dating age." However, it is my opinion that age sixteen is the norm. But, as indicated in a recent letter to *Young Companion* (July, 1989), some communities discourage dating at sixteen.

...In our area the "hands off" way of courtship is upheld, and we also discourage dating before the age of 18. Many of them do wait until they are 18 or older, for which we are grateful.

Anonymous—Reprinted from *Young Companion*

The term "dating" was not used in my former community except in jest. They may use the word "dating" or "date" to mock, or make fun of, a custom held by the outsiders. However, within my community it is customary to use the word "have" rather than "date." That is to say, the young person will be asked, "Whom did you *have* last Sunday?" However, "having" as used in this context does not have any sexual connotations.

Once a young man and woman are going steady, he not only will date her on Sunday evenings but may also appear at her house during the week. On this week night the young man will not make his appearance known until the rest of her family is in bed. That is to say, even if he has to wait at the end of the lane in the cold, he does not appear until all the lights in the house have gone out. However, she will know that he is coming and will be awaiting his arrival. He may toss a small pebble or a kernel of corn against her window to let her know of his arrival but usually the dog's bark will be enough to alert her. Standard equipment for a young man of this age includes a flashlight. By the use of a flashlight, he can also let his female friend know of his arrival.

Usually the young man comes into the house and stays until the wee hours of the morning. If they are serious about one another, they will discuss the upcoming wedding. She will tell him about her dowry which had been started very early in her life and continues until she marries. The dowry usually contains homemade quilts, gifts, silverware and other types of useful things. As previously mentioned, Amish couples work diligently to maintain the secrecy and are seldom, if ever, seen together in daylight before the "banns are published" for their marriage.

As previously mentioned, premarital intercourse is not condoned and should an unmarried couple have engaged in such activity, they will both make a public confession and will be shunned for a period of at least two weeks. As stated before, no stigma is attached to this type of activity and it is not considered among the "worst sins." Also, should she be pregnant the number of months following their marriage and the birth of the child is not really that important. Outside observers (who know of such occurrences) find it difficult to believe the lack of a stigma in such cases.

There is mounting evidence that Old Order Amish females of marrying age far outnumber the men. An Amish writer in a recent issue of *Young Companion* asked why and suggested an answer.

Why So Many Single Girls?

I am surprised that nearly everyone seems to think single girls should readily accept it as God's will that they remain single. There is very little difference in the birth rate between male and female, which shows me that in general it is God's will for each one to have a life companion to love and to respect. What is the reason there are so many single girls left? Is it not because so many of our boys leave our faith in their young days? Now, do you think that is God's will? Are we teaching them the way they should go?

Anonymous—Reprinted from *Young Companion*

Marriage

The entire courtship process is conducted with secrecy, and ideally, it is an admirable feat to keep the seriousness of the relationship a secret until the reading of the banns which are published two weeks prior to the wedding.

The rationale behind the secrecy in courtship seems to not have a definite explanation, but appears to be a traditional pattern. It may be conjectured that such secrecy is in line with avoidance of using married couples given names in public and disapproval of public displays of affection.

Of course, the neighborhood realizes when a couple has been going "steady" for quite some time that the wedding is approaching. Thus, since there is nothing equal to an engagement the neighbors often look for telltale signs of the approaching marriage. Marriages are generally held on Tuesdays and Thursdays during the months of November and December. These months follow the busy time of the harvest. A good sign of an approaching wedding is when her family plants a larger than usual garden in the Spring.

When a young couple decides they are ready for marriage, the young man follows a secret, strict, formal plan. He will send a middle man again, as he did while dating, to the bride-to-be parents, who subsequently asks for her hand in marriage. Her parents will already have been alerted and the middle man is simply a traditional formality. However, the middle man always makes his approach in extreme secrecy and will travel to the bride-to-be's home after dark. Once the girl's parents have consented to the marriage, the ministers are involved. They travel to the homes of both youths and counsel with them. Their traveling is also done in secrecy usually following darkness.

If either the middle man or the ministers are seen traveling to the respective homes, the rumors spread quickly. If the two sets of parents, the ministers, the middle man and the two people to be married can maintain this secret until the banns are publicly published, the couple has "pulled one off on the community." Should the plans be found out before the banns are published, the young couple will be visited and noisy shiverreeing of both of their homes takes place. The young man is considered somewhat of a hero if he can maintain this secrecy. The fact that people in the community did not learn of the wedding plans is talked about for many months and maybe even years.

Following the announcement of the upcoming marriage, the couple begins the big plans. The "published" bridegroom may move in with her parents until the wedding. He is highly involved in getting the house cleaned up, especially on the outside, and also in readying the barn for games and so forth. Also, he will help to whitewash the trees and will paint different buildings. As previously mentioned, whitewashing with a mixture of lime and water is a common beautifying activity among the Amish. The trees will be whitewashed from the ground up to about six feet. Also, during these two weeks the bridegroom has the job of calling personally on all those people he and his bride-to-be plan to invite to the wedding reception. In a large community such as ours, not everyone was "called" to weddings. Thus, it was quite an honor to be "called," especially to one being held in a neighboring church district within your settlement. Of course, all the relatives are "called" first. No "call" is official until the bridegroom has invited you personally. The mail may be used to invite people from a distant community. Anyone may attend the ceremony; however, you must be ofically "called" to the wedding reception.

The uncles and aunts of the bride and bridegroom become the cooks for weddings. It is a special honor to be asked to cook since the Amish are traditionally known as great cooks. The cooks will appear at the future bride's house a couple of days before the wedding and begin baking pies, cakes, homemade noodles and so forth. A custom held in most Amish communities is for the bridegroom to kill the chickens for the wedding feast. Conspicuously absent in an Amish wedding or preplanning of the wedding is flowers and/or corsages of any type.

The bridegroom invites several of his close male friends or relatives to become the *hostlers*. These are the young men who help unhitch the guests' horses as they arrive. The wedding ceremony usually begins around nine o'clock in the morning and may last up until 1:00 p.m. or after. The service begins with the bride, usually dressed in a simple home sewn ankle length robin-egg blue dress, and bridegroom, dressed in black or dark gray, along with their attendants, meeting upstairs or in the basement with the bishops, deacons, and ministers of the church. During this time the congregation sings hymns. Although the attendants and the waiters are upstairs, they will not be in the same room with the couple to be married and the religious leaders. During the time the couple and the leaders are upstairs, they discuss the multifold responsibilities and obligations of an Amish Christian marriage.

Following an hour or so, the bishop, deacons and ministers, along with the couple and wedding party, resume their seats in front of the men in the living room of the house. One of the deacons delivers the initial sermon (in German) and refers often to Biblical references regarding the obligations of marriage. Following this initial sermon there are several minutes of kneeling in silent prayer. Then the bishop delivers the main wedding sermon. The wedding couple has nothing to say about the service. That is, nothing that happens will have been dictated by them. Also, the parents of both will have had little to say about the plans and are simply guests like others. The parents of neither will have been given any kind of special attention at the wedding or reception that follows.

Following the long wedding ceremony all those who had been given a "call" return to the home of the bride. Some who come bring a gift which may range from small pigs to saws or hammers for the bridegroom and cooking utensils and so forth for the bride. In many Amish communities names are not attached to gifts and no written "thank you" is expected.

After returning to the home of the bride the wedding party takes its place in a specially designed corner of the dining room. The tables will have been previously decorated with wedding cakes and other imaginative desserts. Usually these have been prepared by girlfriends of the bride or by the cooks. To be selected as a "carver" or a table waiter for a wedding is a distinct honor. There is always much speculation (some may say "gossip") as to who will be the carver and the waiters for an approaching wedding.

In some Amish communities it is a custom for the young unmarried men to form a group, pick up the bridegroom and toss him over the fence into the waiting arms of a group of young married men. Although this custom was not necessarily done at all the weddings in my community, I have witnessed it several times. This is called the expulsion of the "benedict." Symbolically, this is a transition from the carefree bachelorhood to the life of the Amish married man with the many related responsibilities.

Eating is an important activity of all present at the wedding. Eating occurs throughout the afternoon and usually up until 10:30 p.m. or midnight.

In most communities the young man and his wife will spend that night in an upstairs room at the bride's parents' home. There is nothing equivalent to a honeymoon in the Amish tradition. However, the newly married couple will spend the next couple of weeks visiting in the homes of their relatives. Here they will pick up additional practical gifts. Some Amish do refer to this as a type of honeymoon.

Following these few weeks of touring the Amish community, the couple will usually return to the home of the groom's father. They will spend some time here and wait for the opportunity to purchase land and/or take over one of the farms of one of their respective parents.

Few women or men remain single. The approximate age of marriage for men is 18 to 22 and for women is 18 to 21. Those women that do remain single cease attending the Sunday night singings (the "crowd") at about 25 or 26 years of age. They remain within the family orientation and usually take over some of the household and child-rearing duties of the mother. Often they work outside the Amish community as maids in local residences or become Amish school teachers. Frequently, these women will later marry older Amish widowers.

Remarriage, following the death of a spouse, is encouraged and is quite common one or two years following the death. The community is quite solicitous in this event and often makes suggestions to the widowed spouse for likely new partners.

I believe that the reader will gain much insight into the lives of young married Amish women of today by carefully reading the following letter which appeared in the July, 1989 issue of *Young Companion*.

Advice for the Young Married Woman

There are a number of tricks to make the old-fashioned way easier, more efficient and more enjoyable.

To begin with, people who have no other stove to cook with except a wood stove, heat their dishwater while they are cooking the meal. This way the fire is not needed for so long. Also, they use "summer" wood which burns quickly, heats well in the process, then dies out. Be sure to heat enough water to refill the dishpan if there are a lot of dishes. Washing dishes in cold water is not fun, and it does a poor job.

Once the meal is past, the dishes, pots, pans, platters and bowls are neatly stacked with the largest at the bottom. A cabinet top near the dry sink serves as counter space, and so does a deep window sill or a table.

Next, put the chunk of homemade soap in the dishpan and pour the hot water over it. (You should use rain water. Hard water doesn't work.) This will produce nice suds, especially if you're using a new chunk of soap. In fact, you will have to remove the soap before very long, or you will have far too many suds.

These suds are so different from detergent suds. Detergent suds are all on top. The suds of homemade soap are mixed in *and* on top of the water, making it nice and soft. Too many suds make the water slippery and slithery, or even slimy. I remember having to scoop suds out by the handful and still there were too many, all because I had left the soap in too long.

But when your chunk is old and small, you can pour hot water over it, swish all you like, and still get barely enough suds. Then it is time for a new chunk of soap.

An inbetween chunk of soap can be left in the water for a while, then removed for a turn, and when the suds grow fewer, put back into the water. Only don't forget to take the soap out before you dump the water. Otherwise, you will have to look for it in the grass and pick off any dirt and blades of grass that stick to it, or give it a good rinse under the pump.

If you have now done all the dishes, please wipe out the sink before you dump the water. You'll want to wring the "sink" water into the dishpan. And before you hang up the dishrag, rinse it in clean water. This will help to keep it from getting slippery.

When every dish has been put away, the sink is dry, the dishpan empty, and the dish rag hung up— how tidy the kitchen looks. And the dishpan can be used to snitz apples, scrub carrots, peel potatoes, you name it.

I'm not yet thirty-five, but I still prefer the old-fashioned way, especially homemade soap.

Anonymous—Reprinted from *Young Companion*

Death

Customs surrounding death and burial vary somewhat from one Amish community to another. Although quite young when she died, I feel that the following account of my own mother's death and burial as I remember it (with the help of my late father) is typical.

*   *   *   *   *

Mom had been complaining of a backache and stomach ache following the birth of my youngest brother. However, the advice of the physicians was sought too late and she died of a ruptured appendix.

My father explained to us children that we would not be seeing mom anymore because she had simply gone to sleep and that she was in heaven with God.

The family was in a quandary concerning a state law which required embalming. However, as dictated by law, the body was taken to a small Catholic funeral director where the embalming was performed. During this first evening the body remained at the funeral home. However, many of the neighbors, aunts, uncles and cousins came to our house making plans for my mom's funeral. News of the death spread quickly throughout our Amish settlement and all during that night relatives and non-relatives visited our home. Amish tradition prevailed and decisions regarding the funeral arrangements were made by relatives. Six of mom's nephews would serve as grave-diggers and pallbearers. Six non-relatives, three males and three females all past age sixteen but unmarried, would serve as the "chore boys and girls" who are customary when death claims an Amish sect participant. These people take over the farm chores and manage the household until two days following the funeral. These young people attend to their duties gladly since being chosen as a chore boy or girl is a sign of distinct maturity and a coveted responsibility among Amish youth.

Even though mom's body was still at the funeral home, the wake continued throughout the night. The chore boys and girls plus relatives and neighbors provided food which was served every six hours around the clock.

Another relative worked throughout the night building a casket—a simple pine box. There would be no concrete vault. The following morning the pine box was taken to the local funeral director and mom's body was then delivered to our house.

We were not confronted with typical decisions faced by the outsiders at such a grieving time. Tradition took care of these decisions. My mother was buried in a simple ceremony in an unmarked grave in an Amish cemetery. There were no flowers of any kind, no tent and no artificial grass at the burial site.

The chore group secured as many helpers as they needed for the preparation of the meals and our Amish neighbors delivered food to our home at all hours. Mom's funeral would be held on the third day following her death, traditional among the Amish.

The casket was placed in my parent's bedroom and a kerosene lamp remained lighted 24 hours a day. The light was dimly lit and I remember the erie shadows cast as people came in and out of the room to view the body. No one sat in this room, but from time to time people would get up from other rooms and walk into the bedroom, view the body and then quietly return to their sitting place in another part of the house. This was indeed a somber occasion.

On the second night of the wake it rained. I remember seeing the constant arrival and departure of dozens of black buggies. Our barnyard turned into a vast mudhole and since top-buggies were not permitted in my community at that time, there was little chance of avoiding the rain. The wet heavy shawls the women wore and the heavy serge material in the males' clothing had a distinct mothball odor when wet.

There were people in every room of our house and they talked in low voices and often visited the wooden casket. They sat around on low flat benches, brought in especially for funeral services, weddings and church services.

Early on the morning of the funeral the buggies began to arrive again. As the buggies arrived, the men and boys unhitched the horses and tied them to a wooden fence around our barn lot. Women and children moved slowly toward the house which was gradually and quietly filling. The women hung their heavy black shawls and bonnets on the clothes line before entering the house. Married men and small boys stopped to remove their overshoes on the porch and then filed in to take their places in the living room. The young, unmarried women (sixteen years of age or over) took their usual places behind these married men to the rear of the living room. The married women remained in the dining and kitchen area along with the younger children. The upstairs quickly filled with younger men and some older ones who had not found a place in the living room. Hundreds of people were left standing outside the house. They crowded close to the windows which by now had been opened slightly so as to hear the preaching services. The ministers, eight in all, were seated in front of the living room group facing the married men while the casket sat between the two groups. At 9:00 a.m. the first minister stood and began delivering a sermon such as one would hear on an ordinary Sunday at an Old Order Amish church service. He used this emotional occasion to plead with all the young people present to follow church (to follow church means to take instructions for six weeks and become a member if sixteen or beyond) and lead a life such as my mother had led. In about an hour, the second minister stood to preach the main sermon. His approach was also personal and direct. Several outsider friends of my mother were present and from time to time the ministers repeated themselves in English. Following about an hour of preaching, the second minister asked everyone to leave the living room so that the ministers could arrange the casket for the final viewing. The casket would not be opened at the grave site. At this point everyone returned to their seats and the third minister delivered a short obituary after which everyone kneeled for a long prayer. Then, all present formed a line and viewed mom for the last time. The men moved to the barnyard and began hitching their horses to the buggies and began lining up for the long trip to the Amish cemetery.

The hearse was one of our regular two-horse wagons with three spring- box type seats pushed forward. The casket was pushed into the wagon and, due to the three foot sideboards, was visible only to my family and me sitting in the seats above the casket. Dad told me that more than 100 buggies, pulled by horses in a narrow, curved line followed our hearse wagon that fateful day.

The cemetery, a small, plain field located in the midst of the Amish community, does not have gravestones such as are seen in modern cemeteries. Unaware outsiders do not realize that a cemetery is even located there.

Upon our arrival at the cemetery, the horses were left hitched to the buggies and were tied to the cemetery fence. The casket was moved to the grave and secured by two hickory poles placed over the grave site previously dug by six of my relatives. Following a few words by the bishop, the service ended and the gravediggers, using wide belt straps, lowered the casket into the ground. One man descended into the grave and taking shovelfuls of dirt from above handed to him by other gravediggers, gently and slowly placed dirt on the casket. After the casket was covered with a thin layer of dirt, the man left the hole in the ground to join the other gravediggers who quickly filled the grave. At this point everyone turned to leave the grave for the journey back to our home where all again would eat.

The only outsider present at the grave side services was the undertaker. I remember as we were slowly making our way back to my home how the undertaker's black car sped past our buggies. Today, I think about how out-of-place an automobile was on such a sad day for my family.

As we left the cemetery, my father told his family that there would be no reason for us to return to my mother's resting place. She was no longer there, and I have never returned.

Back at our house the community waited for the post-funeral meal. Everyone contributed. There was a large granite bowl of mashed potatoes, fried chicken, a crock of sauerkraut cooked in pork broth, noodles, apple pie and plenty of coffee.

The next day my household returned to normality. The grief was not easy; however, it had been made lighter because the entire community had shared it with us. The Amish community always shares the grief of one of its members, whether it be the loss of a loved one through death or through expulsion from the community.

Section V

The Amish Plan of Education

By now it should be obvious to the reader that Amish youngsters are raised very carefully and that rigorous methods are employed to protect them from the contaminating influences of the outsider. And, this is especially true regarding education. If there is a fear among Amish parents, it is the fear of their youth obtaining too much formal education. Formal education, to the Amish, ends with the eighth grade.

A Brief History of the Problems with Public Schools

The Amish are opposed to any formal education beyond the eighth grade, and for most, below that level if it requires attending a modern, consolidated public school. They are opposed especially to the emphasis placed on science, the competitive atmosphere and the alien "outsider" teachers found there. They prefer the old-fashioned, one- or two-room school with its limited facilities, in as much as this type of school is more in keeping with the simple life at home. Although many Amish communities have some type of vocational school for those beyond the eighth grade but not yet of legal quitting age, most prefer to train their youth at home in matters dealing with the care and operation of farms and farm households.

Contrary to popular belief, Amish schools are on the increase in the 1990s. The 1972 *Amish Teacher Directory* listed the names and addresses of only 329 Amish schools in the U.S.A. with around 5,000 students enrolled. This directory also listed the founding date of each school and more than 90% had been founded since 1968. Now, in 1990 there are 719 Old Order Amish schools in America alone—a growth of 100% in only twenty years! Old Order Amish students now number more than twenty thousand, all in grades one through eight. The large majority of the teachers in the Amish Schools, approximately 720, are themselves Old Order Amish, they are themselves eight grade graduates and not "teacher" certified by the states they teach in.

The Supreme Court's banning of prayers in the public schools, the emphasis on science and evolution, the increase of violence and drug usage in America and educational television were among the major factors for the sudden increase in the number of Amish schools during the late sixties and early seventies. Amish parents contend that, according to the *Bible*, their children belong to them and thus are not to be educated by the state nor for the benefit of the state. Anything taught beyond the three Rs is a waste of time. Educational television, school pictures, competitive sports, gym classes with scanty uniforms and pledges of allegiance are among the many "godless" features banned from the Amish schools.

The Amish adults realize that public school teachers strive to instill a love of learning in their charges. And, when Amish children do attend public schools, they are good, obedient, hardworking students, and well-liked by their teachers. These teachers, out of compassion, often impose their values on Amish children and strive to alter their perceptions of life. Admittedly, this is usually an unconscious effort on the part of the teacher, but its intent is just as deadly to the Amish way of life. Compassionate non-Amish individuals such as teachers often look upon the Amish youth as deprived and thus try to be "helpful," but are often harmful.

I can vouch for the dissonance and psychological pain endured by Amish youth in a public elementary school. One who has never been a member of a distinct minority group surrounded by the majority can never fully realize the notion of being "different." The two forces—the internalized Amish values and the dominant culture's values—antagonize one another constantly. Put yourself in the Amish child's place in the following school situations: 1) The non-Amish children in the class see an educational film with the teacher's assurance that it is worthwhile and educational; however, you have been taught that it is sinful to view any film and you leave the room so as not to be contaminated. 2) You are told by the teacher that it is truly American to salute the flag and to pledge allegiance, but as the other children stand to do so, you must remain seated because the *Bible* says, "Have no other Gods before me." 3) Your teacher indicates that fighting for your country is American and the non-Amish youth are constantly talking about what branch of the service they will someday join; however, you realize that as a conscientious objector, you will never go to war. 4) As an assignment, you are to talk about your favorite cartoon character, but you have never seen a television set and your parents do not subscribe to the daily newspaper. And, (5) your first language is German and you are constantly reminded to speak English. Literally dozens of similar situations could be cited. Thus, it is no wonder that Amish children, as indicated below, are leery of non-Amish schools and "glad I go to our school."

No Public School for Me

In public school they teach worldly stuff that isn't good for Amish children. I once talked to an English girl and she told me they see picture shows and cartoons in school. She told me about one picture show about a haunted house. It was scary just hearing her tell it. I'm glad I go to our school....

Ruth, fifth grade

In addition to the above, Amish parents are especially concerned about the consequences of their offspring's association with the "outsider" children in the public school. The parents realize that their children would acquire needs which cannot be satisfactorily fulfilled within the confines of the Amish culture.

The average American school is especially congruent with middle-class attitudes and the teachers' main objective is to transmit this cultural heritage to American youth. This objective frightens the God-fearing Amish who do not want their children attaining, nor even being exposed to, many of today's American values. They fear that modern education overemphasizes science, technology and violence.

The Amish always have opposed sending their children to the public high schools, but many Amish were not that opposed to the public elementary schools until the late sixties and early seventies. The Amish leaders realized at that time in their history that the sect's survival was at stake if their youth continued to attend any type of public school, and they took action to stop the practice. They believed, as they do today, that the education obtained there was irrelevant and would only alienate the Amish children against their culture and parents. Thus, they began to develop their own schools with a curriculum (and surroundings) they felt would best meet the needs of the Amish society. These schools, developed in each of the twenty states then inhabited by the Old Order Amish, ran into difficulty with the state and local educational authorities in most every state. A major confrontation resulted between the Amish and the educational authorities because of the Amish sect's desire to employ their own eighth-grade graduates as teachers. However, the biggest and most threatening problem with the state and local school authorities focused on Amish children who were beyond the eighth grade but not yet of legal quitting age. The Amish felt these children should be considered finished with their formal education. However, they were being forced to go to high school until they were of legal quitting age. The Amish usually do not balk at rules and laws unless they are very opposed to them. And, they were very much opposed to sending their children on to high school and many, many Amish parents served jail sentences as a result.

To this writer there was no doubt that America's emphasis on education in the late sixties and early seventies, especially high school education, was threatening the Old Order Amish sect's values and way of life. And, I knew that something had to change or (in my opinion) the Amish would disappear from America. The nonconforming Amish were having difficulty with several innovative aspects of the dominant American society that surrounded them at that time in their history; however, none seemed as insurmountable as their predicament regarding modern, compulsory high school attendance for their youth. This unwanted education being imposed on them was causing many Amish youth to leave the sect and many Amish families to leave America in search of religious freedom!

Literally hundreds of cases of Amish parents being fined and/or placed in jail for refusing to send their children to high school could be documented. There are even documented cases of Amish children being legally taken from their parents, placed in children's homes and forced to attend high school. In another highly publicized case, Amish children were forced into school buses by sheriff's deputies and driven to a local high school. Then, on May 15, 1972 a dramatic event occurred—the National Committee for Amish Freedom, on behalf of the Amish, won a unanimous U.S. Supreme Court decision exempting them from state laws compelling their children to continue schooling beyond the eighth grade. In essence, the court indicated that compulsory, formal education beyond the eighth grade would greatly endanger, if not destroy, free exercise of the Amish religious beliefs.

The ruling affirmed a 1971 judgment by the Wisconsin Supreme Court, first in the country to protect the Amish from school attendance laws. Legal scholars indicate that this is the first time in the history of America that compulsory education laws have been successfully challenged. And, to this date, no other group has been successful in this regard.

The case involved three Wisconsin Amish fathers who were fined a symbolic five dollars each for refusing to enroll their adolescent children in the local public high school.

The Supreme Court ruling meant that the Amish, who had always considered formal education past the eighth grade to be sinful, could no longer be forced by any state authorities to continue schooling beyond that level.

As vice-chairman of the National Committee for Amish Religious Freedom, the organization defending the "defenseless Christian" in this battle, and as a former member of the Old Order Amish sect, I was personally relieved and gratified by the ruling. Having grown up Amish for the first sixteen years of my life, I found it hard to realize that day in 1972 that this conflict was finally over. I remember well the turmoil in my community each time an Amish child, beyond eighth grade but not of legal quitting age, was forced into high school. Some of the Amish leaders had worked out an agreement with local public school teachers so that Amish children would purposely be failed in the eighth grade and thus would repeat the grade until they were of legal quitting age. Other parents, including mine, held their children out of elementary school until age eight so that they would be sixteen (the legal quitting age in most states) upon completion and never enter the local, contaminating high school. The local school authorities usually "winked" at this practice and seldom forced the issue.

In retrospect, it has always been clear to me that the American high school could in no way transmit the values needed by an Amish youth to remain Amish. The public high school generally prepares its students for college, whereas the post elementary education plan proposed by the Amish prepares their children for Amishhood, for life as God-fearing Amish people. The Supreme Court decision made this possible.

The Amish Schools Today

Following the Supreme Court decision, the Amish reached agreements with the state school authorities in every state in which they lived. Some states agreed to a high school equivalent education for all their Amish parochial school teachers. This high school education requirement is met by taking the high school equivalent General Educational Development (GED) test and obtaining a minimum score set by the respective state. The first of these tests, administered by the writer and State of Indiana educational officials, were given to over 70 Old Order Amish males and females and yielded some of the highest scores ever recorded for the GED in Indiana. More than 75% passed the first examination and were then qualified to teach in the Amish schools. Some of those taking the tests were as young as sixteen; others were beyond sixty years of age.

Each Amish community elects an all male school board and several states have elected state level executive school boards, also all male. None of these officials will have graduated from high school. The local boards literally run their local school and their word is final. And, it is their duty to see to it that the teacher is doing a good job. Board members often visit the school when in session and take their job very seriously.

The Amish have agreed to two semesters of instruction in reading, writing, spelling and arithmetic. A minimum of one semester of instruction is taught each year in both geography and history. All courses must be taught utilizing the English language. German, the Amish child's first language, may be taught as a subject at the option of the local school board. In many Amish schools one afternoon a week is set aside for German lessons taught with the help of interested parents (The writer was present during one of these community instruction periods and observed ten parents instructing 31 students). Science, art, shop and organized physical education are not a part of the curriculum and there are few extracurricular activities. No textbooks are used except those recommended by the Amish school boards and many are hand-me-downs from the local public school system. Some Amish elders and others, will, from time to time, suggest that the teachers use only German in all instruction. However, I know of no Amish school where this occurs. The Amish realize that they must do business with their non-Amish, English speaking neighbors and that they must, as stated in the following essay, "**teach English.**"

We Must Teach English

We live in an English speaking country. Our textbooks are printed in English. The English language is very much a part of our surroundings. Most parents learned it in public school, but where will our children learn it? They will have to learn it, too, in school—parochial school. And the best way for them to learn it is to have them speak it. Learning a language takes practice, and eight years in parochial school is a good place to practice. The result should be that by graduation the children will have a good enough command of English to be able to deal sufficiently with the society around them.

Once the teacher has the backing of her school board and parents for an "English at all times" rule, one problem yet remains—how to enforce it. Perhaps the solution is to grade. Children are graded in written English grammar, why not also grade them for their ability to speak correctly? Somewhere on the report cards the teacher should type ENGLISH (spoken) and place a mark there each grading period. Not only should children receive a grade for their ability to use English in conversation during classtime, a teacher could even make tests which the pupils would answer, not in writing, but orally. In this way she will be able to determine the student's ability to handle English.

Text books, bankers, salesmen, neighbors, newspapers—our surroundings are filled with English. In some situations a reading ability is needed, in others a writing ability, and others a speaking ability. All three—reading, writing and speaking—go hand in hand in learning a language. With a little extra effort our parochial schools will have the proper balance.

Anonymous—Reprinted from *Blackboard Bulletin*

After successfully completing the eighth grade, and not having reached the age of sixteen, pupils in some Amish school systems enroll in the vocational division. In some systems the vocational students attend school at least one day (five hours) per week during the regular school year until legal quitting age, usually fifteen or sixteen. During this didactic experience they discuss their vocational projects and attend classes in history, general business, mathematics, English and spelling. I am familiar with one system where the vocational students are required to work a minimum of four hours a day on their projects when not in school. Much of the obligation for the vocational plan is put upon the shoulders of the Amish parents. Parents are involved deeply with their school and often visit the premises. The writer was present at an annual state-wide all day school meeting where over 200 Amish adults, mostly men, were in attendance. This number may not seem in excess; however, if one considers that the meeting was held on a weekday during the hay season and that the adults had to come long distances in horse-drawn buggies, it is amazing!

The vocational project areas usually include livestock and poultry, fruits and vegetables, grains, tools, horse-drawn farm equipment, carpentry, homemaking, gardening and so forth. All projects are in regard to the farm and home. However, in some systems, services outside the home may be classified as projects if done in cooperation with neighbors, after obtaining the consent of the parents and the vocational instructor. The projects are supervised by the vocational teacher from beginning to end and it is emphasized that daily chores and routine household duties are not to be considered as vocational projects. Parents are required to keep tabs on the progress of projects and must sign all reports turned in by their respective vocational students.

The Amish educational methods are valid in that they fulfill the needs of the Amish culture. If education is judged by its achievements, the Amish may have one of the most effective instructional systems in the world today. And, the Amish vocational school is itself a major adaption, the first formalized instruction beyond the eighth grade the Old Order Amish have ever been willing to accept. And, it works for them!

The writer has visited many of the Amish parochial schools and has spent several hours in observation of Amish teachers. Previous to the development of their schools, all Amish were farmers and/or farmers' wives; thus, the Amish teachers place great value on teaching as an occupation and on their ability to teach writing, reading and arithmetic. Teachers are held in high esteem and it is an honor to be a teacher. Admittedly, these teachers have not gone beyond the eighth grade formally, but to categorize them as high school "dropouts" would be unjustifiable and a misnomer. They are grounded fully in the Amish doctrines, and are selected because of their spiritual well-being, resourcefulness, efficiency, and especially, their motivation. Many of the Amish teachers receive the equivalent of a high school diploma via correspondence schools. In this manner of educating themselves, they retain their basic philosophy of remaining "apart from the world."

Anyone visiting the Amish schools will observe efficient teaching methods being utilized and true learning taking place in the absence of technology, a red pencil and a B.S. degree! The Amish teachers teach reading, writing and arithmetic with tender loving care. These teachers, because of the familial and cultural training received, refrain from harsh, coercive methods and use group praise abundantly. Their cultural background predetermines non-aggressiveness, and the assertive, punitive approach to education is not observed in the Amish schools. The teacher and "scholars"—as Amish pupils are referred to—are on a first name basis, and are often related. Modern educators who learn of this often reveal their amazement at such mannerisms and are concerned about respect and discipline. However, Amish teachers have few disciplinary problems with their "scholars."

The basic reason for the absence of serious discipline problems is the children's respect for authority, the real involvement of the parents and the Amish instructor's belief that they are guides, rather than teachers, in the formation of the Amish child's life.

My Teacher

...I like Mary, our teacher. She is nice, kind and a Christian. I went to school with the English my first two years and didn't like it. They were so loud and my first teacher was loud too. She had her fingers painted and her lips were very red. She scared me one day. I like Mary best. She is my cousin....

Rebecca, fourth grade

There is a conspicuous absence of the critical and analytical methods of teaching in the Amish schools and memorization is the major learning technique utilized. The Amish society is such that few things are written (seldom even the rules of the church) and the Amish teachers realize the importance of memorization to a participant of such an oral-traditional culture. They teach their charges to be mild, unquestioning, nonaggressive and obedient. They do not foster the development of creativity nor innovativeness.

Most of the Amish schools utilize two academic teachers—one for grades one through four and another for grades five through eight. The teachers often have teaching aides and utilize the older students in tutoring roles extensively. The teaching salary, paid from an assessment of the Amish church members, varies from $15 to $20 per day and may include payment for the janitorial chores which often accompany the teaching duties. Both male and female teachers could make considerably more money if employed elsewhere. Females working as "maids" for outsiders make more money than do the Amish teachers. And, the same can be stated for Amish male carpenters. Teachers obviously love their work.

The following excerpts, taken from the September, 1989 issue of the *Blackboard Bulletin*, are statements made at an Amish Midwestern School Meeting.

"Show your teacher your appreciation. Give her a raise at mid-term."

"Killing a mosquito with a sledge hammer gets an overkill."

"God likes small people—He cannot use big ones."

"I shoe horses for a living. It's hard work, but I would not shoe horses for the wages a teacher gets."

"With slow learners, tell them what you are going to say, then say it, then tell them what you said."

"All good things go to ruin if we don't work on them."

"The effort to catch the foxes that ruin our schools begins within ourselves. We cannot catch our neighbor's foxes."

"We can't teach a dog anything unless we know more than the dog."

"Teachers are human, and humans all have something in common—they at times have a problem with the capital letter 'I'."

"The electric chair is not the solution to crime, but the high chair."

"Our schools cannot be better than the homes the children come from."

"School is like a threshing machine; one small part can disrupt the function of the whole works."

Anonymous—Reprinted from the *Blackboard Bulletin*

One of the more noticeable physical characteristics of most Amish school yards is the small barn where the horses are fed and stalled for the school day. The school lots generally are covered with buggies and modern playground equipment is conspicuously absent.

Driving to School

One thing I didn't like about going to outsider school was riding the noisy school bus. Also, sometimes the outsider kids made fun of us Amish. So, there are many reasons why I like having our own schools. But, one reason is getting to drive our horse to school. I feed him at noon and I like this. Also, I couldn't talk English very good in the first grade and sometimes children laughed at me. Here at _____ school I can talk dutch often.

Amos, fifth grade

The school building generally is rectangular in shape and constructed of wood framing covered with clapboard. There is a cupola at the entrance, followed by two sex-separated anterooms for garment hanging. Once inside the main room, one normally sees simple drawings of animals, fruits and vegetables, along with *Bible* verses and aphorisms decorating the walls. The students sit at desks which, in many cases, have been discarded from a public school classroom. There are neither window curtains nor electric lights, and a potbellied stove adorns a corner of the room. It is evident that the physical aspects of the school, along with the curriculum, coincide with the Amish values and ways.

Many comments, some rather strongly worded, have been made by educational experts regarding the use of eighth-grade graduates as Amish teachers. Educational authorities often believe that these teachers are inadequate and that the Amish students will not learn. However, it is my professional opinion that the Amish school system works. The teachers take their jobs seriously and do a good job. And, the Amish schools are teaching what Amish parents want their children to know and learn. The tenacious Amish utilize their schools to maintain their cultural integrity and uniqueness as a minority group. I sincerely believe that if the Amish had not been permitted their own schools, they would have become extinct to America in a short time.

More could be written about the Amish plan of education and more reasons could be given, both by myself and the Amish, concerning the positive aspects of the Supreme Court's decision permitting the Amish to have their own unique plan of education. What does it mean? It means the Amish with their unique ways can remain unique. It is not only legitimate now to be an Amishman in America, it is also legitimate to be educated as one. As written elsewhere in this book, many Amish people left American because of persecution and cited the school problem as a basic reason for their departure. But, the court decision has practically stopped the Amish exodus to Central and South America.

Section VI

Problems in the 1990s

What Will the 1990s Bring?

...Sometimes I wonder what the world is coming to. Everybody in the outsider community seems to be in a hurry when you meet them. I read in the papers that this is why they have so many heart attacks. They are no longer satisfied with cars and airplanes as they are building rockets to ride in. Will they ever be satisfied? For me the buggy is quick enough....

Amos, sixth grade

How long will civilization go along with the Amish? How long can the Amish with their closed society housed within a highly progressive, secular society survive? It is my belief that the Amish will survive and maintain their distinctiveness so long as they can keep the figurative wall between themselves and the secular society. Failure to maintain this wall brought about the disappearance of the Amish in Europe and the same could occur in America.

Urbanization is threatening the Amish way of life. This is especially true as farming becomes more mechanized and real estate developments send up the price of land. The economic problems of a people committed to a primitive technology, but imbedded in a highly technological society with which it must make exchanges across system lines, are immeasurable. For example, one of the Amish farmer's largest economic supplements is the selling of fluid milk to the local dairies. However, the new laws and demands of milk inspectors have made it almost impossible for an Amishman to continue to sell milk to the local dairies. Many Old Order Amish farmers have gone along with the new type milk parlors and gasoline engine operated cooling systems, but the notion of milking machines is not compatible with the Amishman's belief in non-conformity. But, the milk buyers no longer wish to buy milk that has been produced by "hand." Further, the Amish have continually refused to allow their milk to be picked up on Sunday and dairies want the Amishmen's milk seven days a week or not at all. Many more such farm-related examples could be cited.

The Amish settlements most threatened by urbanization are those that are close to large metropolitan areas. However, Amish communities are faced with the spread of urban life from even smaller cities. Many Amish farms are selling for $1,000 or more per acre. And, if they are close to large metropolitan areas, they will often go for $3,000 to $4,000 or more per acre. Amish farmers usually out-bid their non-Amish neighbors for land within the settlement. However, $300,000 or more is much more than they can afford to pay for 100 acres, the amount of acreage considered necessary for making a living at general farming. In some areas, Amish are cooperating to buy farms by providing each other interest free loans. And in response, more and more "outsider" farm auctions are being held on Sunday, eliminating the cooperative Amish bidders. Thus, many of the Amish people have found themselves dividing their acreage into much smaller plots and taking jobs in industry on the side. Many hundreds have left the United States in search of "new lands"—a Biblical dictate to do so if they "continue to stop up your wells."

Many Amish farmers have practically given up farming during the last ten or fifteen years. Some have maintained a small farm for cattle and pasture to graze their driving horses while turning to traditionally approved occupations of masonry and carpentry—building homes and furniture for the "outsider." However, many are now going to work in church-approved factories which in the past was strictly taboo.

Industrial work is a departure from tradition made necessary by the changing economy. Factory hours are shorter and pay checks are higher. In time factory work will no doubt erode some of the values the Amish have so long treasured. Factory work is especially detrimental to the close knit Amish family organization. It is obvious from the following excerpts from letters (written by Amish mothers) to *Family Life* that the Amish realize this deterioration better than anyone.

Factory Work

...How can a father fulfill his duty when he is away from home all day? My husband worked in a factory for three years and I can see now where he and the oldest boy lost out on a father and son basis by having the boy farming alone mostly. He was too young for such a responsibility. Of course, I tried to help him along as best I could but with other children to care for, he was left alone too much of the time. Now that he is older, he has gone on his own. Please be patient for your boys need your love and fatherly help while they are young. Before you realize it they will be big enough to help and then things will go better....

...Don't you think you can live a closer life to God on the farm? I'm afraid the factories are leading good men farther and farther away from God. Which is the more important, money or a soul? Would you not rather lose everything you have than to lose your soul? And how about the precious souls of your boys?

...I would like to add a word of warning to the fathers who are working away day after day and are not at home with their family. They are not teaching their sons how to work so how will these sons learn to like to work when they grow up? What will it come to? If their sons don't learn to work while young, they will grow up and when they have a family of their own it's the family that will have to suffer. If the head of the family has to push himself to work, there will scarcely be enough to supply his family, let alone all the things his father didn't teach him to do. How can he teach his sons?

Anonymous—All reprinted from *Family Life*

Some Amish churches that changed their "orders" permitting factory work have been known to reverse that decision just as quickly, maybe even the following Sunday! And, many outsider factory owners are perplexed when, because of a new rule made on the previous Sunday, not one of their hard-working Amish men shows up for work on Monday morning!

In the past, the Amish farmer has had a lower overhead than his non-Amish neighbor simply because he used horses. The horse drawn equipment also used to cost less which kept his taxes lower. However, with inflation and scarcity, this type of equipment is increasing in price every day. Also, an Amish farmer never accepts a subsidy of any type from the government. Thus, an Amish farmer seeing his non-Amish neighbor accepting government subsidy for not growing a particular crop, for example, has difficulty understanding such a concept and it can become highly stressful.

As noted above, urbanization and progress has brought about a change for many Amish men. However, it is also changing the lifestyles of many Amish females. There have always been a few young men leaving the Amish church, but now some young women are following suit. In the past, a woman leaving the Amish church was almost unheard of. Why this sudden shift? Most Amish elders blame it on "working out" in modern outsider's homes or in factories. When young women work for another Amish family, they earn between $35.00 and $50.00 a week. However, they learn quickly that they can earn the same amount in one day by doing housework or factory work in town.

Losing a member to the outside world causes tremendous grief for the person's family, the church and other members of the community. The following letter, written in response to a July, 1988 article in *Family Life* entitled "**One is a Big Number**," depicts just how great the grief can be.

One Is Indeed Big

After reading the article, "One Is A Big Number" (July), I felt moved to share our experience. As parents of a large family, we have also felt the loss of a son, only in a different way. Yes, one space is empty. The shirt and the shoes are still here—abandoned for worldly clothes. Ah, yes, in the quietness of a summer's night one hears a car roaring in the distance. It might be him. We also cry, "Oh, God, all the pleading admonitions, the prayers, are they all in vain? Can such a sorrow also bring joy?"

Through earnest prayer we have obtained peace, but are still struggling. Yes, one is a big number.

Anonymous—Reprinted from *Family Life*

Even though some Amish people may enjoy working in factories, they find many requirements there that are contrary to their religion. For example, many industries require that their workers be unionized. This is strictly forbidden by Old Order Amish church rules and is causing tremendous conflict for many Amish people and factory owners alike. Although this may sound trivial, a very important aspect of an Amishman's garb is his black felt hat. This black hat is an important symbol of his religion. However, in many factories Amish men are required to wear hard hats. The church forbids this and many Amish men are losing their jobs as a result.

Young Amish women are also "working out" in record numbers. And, as an Amish person wrote recently (December, 1989), **"I think it would be a good standard not to allow such outside jobs."**

A Finger in the Fire

I was thankful to see the story, "The Path of Temptation." The message is much needed, especially in a community where many girls work out for "English" people. Some may think the girls can be a good influence on their employers, but it usually turns out the other way—usually the young person is the one to be influenced, and not for good. They may soon see no harm in Christian radio programs, even though so-called Christian rock music and hymns, and truth and falsehood are mixed and aired. If you put your finger to the fire, it will get burnt. From experience, I know the evils of TV are very great. No mother in her right mind would let her young daughter take a baby-sitting job if she knew what temptations and evils the girl may be faced with daily.

Also, when you walk into an Amish home you can often detect if the girls (or even the mother, in earlier years) have worked in a worldly home, just by observing how the house is dolled up. Also, such girls often tend to be fence crowders in church. So overall, I think it would be a good standard to not allow such outside jobs. Or at least get the church's consent before making an exception.

Anonymous—Reprinted from *Young Companion*

Some Amish communities permit tops on their buggies (but not for the unmarried) while others do not. The three-cornered slow moving vehicle sign, visible in this illustration, has caused much concern and consternation for many Amish people. Many have served jail sentences for refusing to affix the gaudy orange sign to the backs of their buggies. They feel that the bright colored sign will draw attention to man and away from God. And, since the sign is also required on tractors and other" worldly" machinery, many refuse to use it fearing they will be in conflict with the Biblical dictate, "Be ye not unequally yoked with non-believers."

Although the school controversy, as stated in the previous section, was one of the basic reasons for the emigration of several thousand Amish to South America, there are other more eminent ones. Impingement and persecution come from several different sources. Local, state and national legislators often pass new laws without the consent, knowledge or consideration of different minority groups. A case in point is a law that has passed in several states requiring a triangular-shaped, reflectorized emblem to be affixed to the back of all slow-moving vehicles (the SMV). The Amish, in most states, view this three-cornered gaudy orange emblem as a hex symbol, or "the mark of the beast" as described in the *Bible* and have refused to affix it to their buggies. They further believe that the colorful emblem would glorify man rather than God. The Amish offer to use neutral colored reflector tape in an attempt at compromise, but often fail and end up serving jail terms. Many times compromises are reached. But such compromises are tentative and can change over night with a political change in state or county government. This SMV controversy began almost twenty years ago and, in some localities, remains so.

In general, Americans may feel that Social Security is a good idea. However, it has, in the past, caused immeasurable problems for the Amish who view it as a form of insurance (which is strictly taboo). Many an Amish farmer lost good cattle and horses confiscated by the Internal Revenue Service men during the middle sixties for failure to pay Social Security even though they would never collect a dime of it! There are many documented stories told about this problem. When the IRS men came to an Amish farm to confiscate livestock, the non-aggressive Amish would unselfishly assist them in choosing the livestock they felt would best make up for their lack of paying Social Security. They were always kind to the IRS men and many local newspapers carried stories about these men being taken into the house, given coffee, fed and in one case they loaded the livestock and then went fishing with the Amishman in his farm pond. Other stores reveal how the government men often left with the confiscated livestock with tears in their eyes. However, unlike many other controversies involving the Amish, this one has a happy ending. A rider was attached to the Medicare Bill exempting all Amish people from paying Social Security. However, the problem is now back. The government believes that this legislation does not exempt Amish farmers from paying Social Security for their hired help, even if they are Amish employees!

Local governments often build paved roads through Amish communities which bring fast cars and camera-toting tourists to the Amish farmlands. These roads also play havoc to horses' feet. A horse simply cannot be continually driven on concrete, but local governments have not seen fit to leave grassy strips on either side of the new roads to drive on, explaining the cost as being prohibitive. Also, the Old Order Amish come under continual harassment as they drive along these roads in their open buggies. It is especially popular to harass the young Amish men and their girlfriends as they travel along in their open horse-drawn buggies. Several adults and children have been seriously injured, in more than one case fatally, as the horse bolted after being frightened by passing motorists. One of the most publicized deaths during the 1980s was that of a sleeping infant killed instantly by a piece of asphalt thrown from a passing car. The child was asleep in the rear of the buggy and the parents, unaware that the child had been hit, discovered the death upon reaching their home more than an hour later!

Non-Amish youth frequently invade the Amish communities at night and perform such harassments as turning out livestock, upsetting outdoor toilets and burning corn and wheat shocks. This is especially prevalent during Halloween or when America is at war. These same culprits, realizing that the defenseless Amishman's religion prevents his calling the local sheriff, will pull a buggy behind a car or truck at high speed and release it to crash into bits and pieces against the road bank or tree.

Some Other 1990 Problems

Genetic Problems

Past inbreeding among the Amish, as mentioned previously, is currently a very serious problem and appears to be getting worse as many second cousin marriages continue. In the following article an Amish writer succinctly, and in a scholarly manner, details the problem. He also chastises Amish leaders for not doing more about the problem.

The Laws of Heredity

...In the last twenty years there has been an alarming increase in genetic weaknesses and diseases among the plain communities. Some of these are cystic fibrosis, hemophilia, dwarfism, muscular dystrophy, albinoism and Maple Syrup Urine Disease.

But why should the Amish and Mennonites have more such inherited problems than other people? Is it a special judgment of God upon us? Is it a sign that we are weaker than other people?

No, it is none of these. It is simply the laws of heredity going into effect. It is due to our limited gene pool. Because we tend to marry within our own communities for generations, we become more closely related to each other than the general population. Even those of us who think we are not related to each other often find that if we trace back our family lines, we share a common ancestor or two (p. 11).

...What can be done about it?

Surely the first step is to become aware of the problem. I am often appalled by our lack of even being aware that there is a problem. In one community, where marrying is permitted between first cousins and severe hereditary problems are showing up, a member of the community said, when asked about first-cousin marriages—"Well, I guess it is still better than going out into the world to marry."

In another instance, in a community where in some cases nearly the entire family is confined to wheelchairs, a bishop was heard to remark resignedly, "Well, I always feel that God is sending us these cases to see if we are willing to take care of them."

It certainly is a commendable attitude not to want to marry people who do not share our faith, as it is commendable to care for the crippled and needy. But there is nothing Christian about ignoring the laws of nature that God has fixed and put into place when He created an orderly world. The laws of heredity are a part of that creation, and if we ignore them it is to our own hurt. The best gift we can bestow upon future generations is to make every intelligent effort within our power and ability to ensure that they do not inherit genetic weaknesses from us (p. 11).

...And once we have faced the problem, and become aware that it is a problem, we need to search for some solutions. Since the problem is the result of inbreeding over too many generations, a giant step in the right direction would be to widen the genetic scope of our young people's potential partners. This is especially urgent in those communities where the young people almost never marry outside the home community, and into which no new families move from other communities. This means that generation after generation the young people marry into the same families, with no new genes entering the community. Given enough time, this is almost a sure formula to genetic disaster, and once problems become visible, we have waited plenty long to seek solutions. Church leaders and parents need to recognize that it is important for a community to have genetic diversity. This can be brought about by more interaction between communities in the form of visiting or moving. Welcoming converts from outside our plain circles will also greatly help this problem, though that in itself would be a questionable motive for encouraging converts!

Another step we might take would be to discourage seeking partners who are too closely related. I personally feel it is high time to take another step, and work toward the elimination of second cousin marriages, also.

Yes, I know our forefathers always married second cousins. Which is exactly the reason it may no longer be wise for us to do so!

Another solution that should become apparent to us is to discourage those who have serious genetic weaknesses from marrying, at least during their childbearing years. For when even one partner has the actual weakness, it will be inherited by a given percentage of his or her children. Perhaps I should state this again to make it clearer. When only the gene is defective, both partners need to have the same gene defective, before the disease shows up in the children. If however, a person has the actual defect itself, and gets married, he or she will pass it on to a given percentage of the children. That is why it would seem an act of mercy and prudence for such a person to voluntarily forego the right to marry... (P. 12).

Stoll, E., *Family Life*, Aug.-Sept., 1988

Another Amishman, responding to the above August, 1988 essay in *Family Life*, writes about how his intermarriage (**"our grandparents were related on both sides, our parents were related on both sides, and we were related on both sides"**) caused the birth of two retarded children in his family.

Two Retarded Children

...Do not get me wrong—we take the very best care to provide so that our two retarded children can have it as nice as possible. The one can barely walk any more, and the other one has had several surgeries, in an attempt to improve his walking, but to no avail.

When our first one was born and as soon as it was noticed that the baby was retarded, we got so much advice as to where to go and how this or that person got help. They meant it well. We went to different doctors and also one of the most noted clinics in the United States, all to no avail. It is just as the article stated, if the genes are in both parents, it is like planting corn and hoping to harvest oats. When we married, we were just as unconcerned about genes as I think most other young couples in love are. We did not give a thought that our grandparents were related on both sides, our parents were related on both sides, and we were related on both sides.

In our area there are several family lines especially high in degenerative factors such as mental retardation and "Smallism." Perhaps most people do not realize that a high percent of the dwarfs in the United States are Amish, without a doubt due to inbreeding.

We have in our area several large families where the parents are second cousins. Some of the children are quite short and have other distinctive features. In our particular church area most of the people are related to each other, if you trace back four or five generations.

Some people say, in an unconcerned manner, that in Biblical times the old patriarchs married close relatives without any apparent adverse effects. Please do not use this excuse in our day or you may be sorry later.

Anonymous—Reprinted from *Family Life*

Most Amish are aware of this very serious problem. However, since the Amish are so inter-related, tend to stay close to home, seldom travel and continue to shun marrying outside the church, it is my opinion that this sect-threatening problem will only get worse before it gets better.

The Problems with Tourists

One of the Amish counties being most threatened by urbanization and progress during the 1990s is Lancaster County, Pennsylvania—the Amish heartland. Civilization is refusing to go along with the Amish in Lancaster and many Amish are leaving it. This is the county first offered as a sanctuary to the Amish by William Penn when he toured Europe.

The several thousand Amish in this beautiful area of Pennsylvania are the target of more than 5,000,000 tourists per year. Tourists travel through the county's back roads in tour buses or sometimes rent buggies and are often a nuisance to the Amish. The Amish write about their tourist problems to the *Budget* and *Family Life* telling of the rudeness of tourists. Recently, an Amish scribe wrote to the *Budget* describing how a busload of tourists trampled his garden in pursuit of a picture of his family as they worked in the garden.

Traveling through Lancaster County one finds an endless string of "Amish" motels, "Amish" food, "Amish" restaurants, "Amish" gift shops, "Amish" museums, "Amish" amusement parks and so forth. This exploitation of the Amish is growing at an alarming pace. Tourism in this one Amish community is now a 100 million dollar plus a year business!

In the winter time, one can travel though Lancaster County going through such tiny Amish villages as Paradise, Intercourse, and Blueballs, which have been left undisturbed for over a 100 years. There one sees the horse and buggy driving Amish, water wheels, windmills and other sights reminiscent of 200 years ago. But, in the summer time the mood changes to a carnival atmosphere as bumper to bumper traffic and billboards indicate that "it's real—it's genuine, you're here. Visit the house and farm occupied by the German-speaking Amish, stop and talk to these genuine Amish people." A tourist's inquisitiveness can quickly become a nuisance to the Amish who strive to avoid publicity and photographs at all costs.

As the following essay indicates, tourists are also often "disrespectful" and even "rude." I urge anyone who plans to tour an Amish community to please read the following very carefully.

How I Tried to Get Rid of the Rude

It was a pleasant morning in July. A refreshing rain the night before had put the soil into a nice condition to cultivate. We live beside a state highway and I was working steadily and paying little attention to the usual flow of traffic. I had my mind on my work for as soon as I was finished, I would have some other things to do.

I heard a car slow down and stop in front of me. When I looked up from my work, the woman in the car had her camera turned on me and at that instant it clicked. She waved her hand and drove on.

I was disgusted but when I thought of the picture which the woman had gotten, it almost amused me. A plump, barefooted woman, red in the face from the heat, with an old, not-too-clean dress on, pushing a hand cultivator. But the vegetable and flower plants looked nice so maybe her picture wasn't too bad after all . This woman hadn't asked permission, she simply took the picture and went on.

I wished she would have asked permission, but I've learned that even though some ask, they don't intend to respect your wishes. For example, last summer I went to a shopping center with my daughter-in-law. She went in first and when I came in, she warned me, "There's a lady in here who says she's from Switzerland and she's taking all the pictures she can get. When she asked me to take mine, I said no, but she just watched her chance and took it anyhow."

The lady was standing by the entry doors which faces the hitching racks and was taking pictures of people putting their groceries on the buggies. This woman asked permission but when it wasn't granted, she took them anyhow. In a way, this seemed even ruder than not asking in the first place.

But the most unpleasant experience I ever had with photo hunters was several years ago. The reason it was so unpleasant was because this time it was not just the tourist that was rude. I had my horse hitched to the surrey and had 4 or 5 of the children with me and was going to my sister's house. My nerves were tense as I turned north for I always dreaded this one mile on a U.S. highway. "Well," I tried to console myself, "surely the factory workers have all gone to work already so there shouldn't be so much traffic on the highway now."

It wasn't too bad and we had gone about half the distance when a car passed me. "Tourists," I said when I saw how they looked back and watched us. Then they turned around and approached us slowly from the rear and I saw they had a camera ready. "Put your heads down," I told the children on the front seat and I also put mine down.

They stopped beside the road in front of us and we passed them and I urged my horse on. I watched for the car to pass us again but they stayed behind us until the highway was clear from both ways. Suddenly the horse jumped and I saw they were passing us on the wrong side. When they were in front of us they suddenly pulled across the road in front of us. I pulled the lines up tight hoping none of the children would slide off the seat because of my sudden stop.

Suddenly I realized they had us where they wanted us. I couldn't put my head down because I had to control my horse and the children were too curious to see what was going on. I felt anger rising up inside me and before I knew what was happening I was yelling at them, "The nerve of some people!" I don't know if I shook my fist or not but at least I almost felt like it.

Of course just at that moment the camera clicked and I could see they greatly enjoyed my annoyance. Right away I felt ashamed of myself. I checked both ways for traffic and drove past without looking at them. They soon went around us again and this time they were laughing and waving their hands mockingly as they sped away.

Just then we turned off the highway and went our way. At first, I felt upset but after I had time to think, I was thoroughly ashamed of myself. What kind of a witness had I been to these people? Would it make them respect the Amish any more? And what did God think of me? Just because they were rude didn't make it right for me to be the same. Maybe their actions didn't look worse to Him under the circumstances than mine did.

When they were crucifying Jesus, causing Him almost unbearable pain, He prayed for them, "Father, forgive them, for they know not what they do." But here I couldn't even take a little mocking and rudeness from these people without getting angry. Maybe God lets things like this happen to try us out. And I have also found out that not all tourists are rude and disrespectful.

Several years ago one evening my husband and I were at the sale of a friend of ours in town. We left our horse at the hitching rack beside the blacksmith shop. I stood beside the buggy and my husband was tying the horse when a car drove in beside us. A man and a woman came out and the woman asked, "Would you mind if we took your pictures standing beside your rig?"

"We'd rather not," answered my husband.

"Thank you," said the lady. "We just didn't know."

We looked the other way and started walking toward the alley. My husband said to me, "They'll probably get us anyway."

I couldn't resist a glance backward and was surprised to see them walking away. They had respected our wishes and didn't take any pictures.

When we happen to have wheat or oats in a field alongside the road, people are always interested in seeing us cut it. The sight of a binder being pulled by four horses, and with someone shocking the grain has stopped many a car. Some only watch but others take pictures. If the threshing machine is operating close to the road, the same thing happens, and they ask to take pictures. These people have never been taught anything different and they use their cameras, somewhat like we use our diary. Where should we draw the line?

Human nature being what it is, I suppose we will always have the politely interested, the curious and the rude people. But I hope, with the help of God, I will never again lose my temper when I meet up with the latter kind.

Anonymous—Reprinted from *Family Life*

Tourism in Lancaster began only 25 or so years ago, but is now a bonanza for the owners. They succeeded well beyond their wildest dreams and today Pennsylvania Dutch country is one of the largest tourist attractions in the United States. As many as 20,000 visitors a day in season swarm down over the Amish back roads. As the above essay verifies, they snap pictures of the Amish whose *Bible* admonishes them not to have "a graven image"—a picture made of themselves. Tourists seldom ask permission to take pictures. They snap pictures from their car windows and also burst uninvited into the easily accessible, quaint, inviting Old Order Amish school houses. The following are short excerpts from letters written (from Amish teachers) to the editors of *Blackboard Bulletin*, the Amish educational journal, about their problems with tourists.

Tourists at School

...Most times tourists seem a nuisance to me, but I guess if I were traveling for pleasure, I would like to travel slowly and ask a lot of questions, too. I do not like it when they take pictures of the children, and I often ask or motion for them to move on. Some do but others are determined to have a picture. I try not to allow the children to call out "no pictures" or to make faces, nor are they to run out to the fence when a car stops. But it seems that it is hard for the little ones just to keep on playing....

...My opinion about tourists in school is the less we have the better off we are. I also feel if we would give them a start there would be no end to it.

...Why do I object to tourists stopping at school? First, it is a distraction to pupils who are supposed to be studying, especially if they come up to the windows and peep in. Some are even bold enough to open the door without knocking. Some are polite enough to knock and ask for admittance, but are so hideously dressed you feel embarrassed at the expression on the pupils' faces when they come in. If they are allowed to come in, they don't seem interested in the school more than for curiosity's sake. I just feel better without them around....

Anonymous—All reprinted from *Blackboard Bulletin*

During the Summer of 1989 the writer experienced the true affects of "Amish Tourism" first hand. I was attending an Amish farm auction, that of a late uncle, when the serenity of the peaceful, horse and buggy environment was suddenly broken by the loud noise of two large Greyhound buses. The dust created by the buses on the non-paved road was tremendous. Both buses came to a stop directly in front of the huge, mainly Amish, auction crowd. All present knew that behind those non-see-through tinted bus windows were many cameras with powerful zoom lenses. Many turned their backs. An Amish cousin, standing next to me, summed up his and my feelings succinctly when he whispered, "It's like we're in a zoo, isn't it?"

The tourism offers practically no benefits to the Amish by their own choice. They are not in the entertainment, nor the hotel and motel business. One of the most damaging aspects of the tourism is that Lancaster County and other Amish settlements have now been "discovered" and the Amish farmers can no more buy more land than they can buy gold. Now, during 1990, there is the possibility that a super highway will be built directly through the center of the Amish heartland in Lancaster. People who are benefiting the most from the Amish leaving the farms are local industry owners. And, if the highway is built, many more will be forced to leave. Amish men and women have been groomed to awaken early in the morning and work is a moral directive. Those now working in non-governmental factories and so forth no longer have to get up so early. And, they make excellent factory workers, but as previously mentioned, often unhappy ones.

Outsiders Wanting In

During the turbulent times of the sixties and early seventies, many non-Amish attempted to "become" Amish. Many were "hippie" types and seldom succeeded. However, the Amish have never closed the door on these types of people whom they refer to as "Seekers." One of the editors of *Family Life* recently wrote about the "**Seekers.**"

The Seekers

...I will admit that for many years I have held a soft spot in my heart for "Seekers"—those people growing up in the world, but longing for better values than they can find in the churches or society around them. More and more of them are coming to the plain people and expressing an interest in sharing our faith and our lives. There are at least two main reasons for this increased number of "Seekers."

1) The plain people are being publicized more and more by the media and the tourist industry. And this is not only being done in North America, but on a global scale, (especially in European countries). More people are interested in the Amish and Mennonites and Hutterites simply because more people know about them than ever before at any time in history.

2) Outside society is steadily deteriorating, and many people are not only disillusioned by secular values, but genuinely depressed and/or frightened. Twenty year ago people still expected progress and education and science to bring in a better world. Today amid the declining morals and accelerating crime, the outlook is bleak. The plain people may not look all that good until you consider the alternatives!

...But anyone today wishing to join the plain people encounters some very real hurdles that must be overcome. We would like to print sometime, hopefully this coming winter, an article on what some of those hurdles are, and provide some pointers for "Seekers." And, of course, such an article should also include some pointers for those of us on the other end—what we can do to make the adjustments easier. Following is a quick list of what some of these hurdles are. Whether you are a "Seeker" who has had some experience (or one who would like to have), or someone who has had experience in helping "Seekers," or merely an interested observer, chip in and give us your thoughts and suggestions.

1) Hurdles related to job and work. Many people in non-plain circles grow up with a different concept of work, or at the best different job skills. For men, it is often an adjustment to learn to do demanding physical labor. Women may have problems with cooking, sewing, canning or gardening.

2) Hurdles related to language. Languages are easy for some people, but difficult for others. Yet to fit into any of the Old Order groups in existence today, German is a must. For those who know the language, it gives them a sense of identity and a feeling of belonging. For those who don't, it can do the very opposite, often right at a difficult stage in the "Seekers" transition.

3) Hurdles related to family and relatives. The plain people put a premium on family ties; a lot of social life revolves around *Freundschaft*. The "Seeker" often finds himself lonely and left out because he has none.

4) Facing reality. We all need some idealism, but the gap between the "Seeker's" expectations of what plain people are like, and what he discovers them to be when he really gets to know them can be a hurdle of considerable size. Some turn back when they find inconsistencies and failings, yes, perhaps even suspicion and unfriendliness toward them personally.

I'm sure another person might list different hurdles, or more. The above four categories are not claimed to be complete; but in my mind they are perhaps the four most common and most serious ones. (Nor are they necessarily listed in order of seriousness!)

Recently there have been at least two different proposals by "Seekers" to establish plain churches especially tailored to the needs of "Seekers." To what extent they will materialize still remains to be seen. This is a development toward which I have mixed feelings. On the one hand I rejoice that at least some-one is actively trying to fill the vacuum, and with concern and compassion provide help for people who are sincerely seeking. On the other hand I am filled with sadness, both for them and for us. We need each other. They need our experience and stability, and we need their idealism, zeal, vision and devotion, not to mention their genes. If we cannot accommodate them in our churches and work together, both of us will be the losers. They will be destined to make mistakes we could have perhaps spared them, and we will continue to be mired with problems they could have contrib-uted toward solving.

Stoll, E., Staff Notes, *Family Life*, Nov. 1989, pp. 7-8

Homosexuality and AIDS

As mentioned elsewhere, I have never heard a discussion among any Amish concerning homosexuality nor have I ever personally heard the word "homosexual" used by an Amish person. Therefore, I was somewhat surprised to find the follow-ing small essay in the March, 1988, issue of *Family Life*. How-ever, as the reader will observe, the term "homosexual" is also not used in the essay. But it appears obvious what is meant by "The Silent Struggle."

The Silent Struggle

...Because of its sins, Sodom was burned by fire. In Romans, Chapter one, Paul calls people who indulge in such sin as worthy of death. Yet today in the world, many people practice this lifestyle. Some estimate as many as ten percent. We pretend this doesn't affect our plain churches. I know differently.

Some people turn to this lifestyle because their lust, given free rein, longs for something different. Many have been this way since childhood; no one knows why.

And our plain society keeps these people hidden, pretending there is no problem, offering no help.

Oh, dear reader, if you are one with this secret struggle, take heart. Your passions can be controlled through the power of God, just like everybody else's passions.

Temptation is no sin; it is the yielding to temptation that is wrong. I don't know why you have this struggle, but maybe God can strengthen your faith through it.

There is hope! Ponder over all the powerful things God has done—creation, the flood, Jesus rising from death—the list could go on and on. Now do you think God can't help you? I believe that if God so wills, He can change your passions so you can be like others. Try to be satisfied though, with whatever seems to be your lot in life, and never yield to living in sin. There is great gain in contentment.

Do not enter marriage just to be socially acceptable; you will hardly be happier and it would be unfair to your partner. Do not marry in hopes of becoming normal. Through the power of God you can be changed, not through marriage. You might find help in books from a Christian bookstore, but beware of all the damaging writings on this subject.

Maybe you do not have this struggle, but have reason to feel one of your friends might have it. Do not just openly approach him about it. He will feel his whole future is being threatened and you will greatly tempt him to lie. Instead, try to grow closer and closer in faith, praying for him, and being truly concerned about him. You may be sure, he is desperate for someone to talk to but he will be fearful of being misunderstood and betrayed.

Anonymous—Reprinted from *Family Life*

Very little has been written about AIDS in the Amish publications. However, based on the very few essays and letters which have appeared, it is my opinion that the following excerpt from a recent letter to *Family Life* (October, 1988) sums up how the Amish feel about AIDS.

...Without sin there can be no AIDS, except in very rare cases. If I personally get AIDS, through a committed sin, I would certainly feel it to be a direct penalty for my sin....

Anonymous—Reprinted from *Family Life*

Out of Touch (on purpose):

The following excerpt from a short essay written by a *Family Life* staff member in June, 1988 reveals how truly out of touch with the "world" one can become without a radio, daily newspaper or television. However, the reader should understand—this is the way the Amish want their lives to be. Their *King James Bible* dictates that they should "remain apart from the world." The "world" begins right past the last Amish farmhouse.

Hostages

Last week one morning I happened to be at the milk house when our milkman came. He knows we don't have a radio, or get a daily paper, so he occasionally shares some world news that he figures might interest me. And that particular morning he announced, "Well, they finally did release those hostages."

I lifted my eyebrows. "Hostages?"

"Yeah, on that plane in the Middle East."

"I'm sorry," I had to admit. "I didn't know a plane was hijacked."

"I figured you had heard," he said. "They've been on that plane for over two weeks—fifty some hostages, including several members of the royal family from the country of Kuwait. They spent a lot of that time grounded in an airport in Cyprus, and couldn't get anyone to refuel the plane."

"What did the hijackers want?" I asked.

"They were demanding the release of seventeen prisoners held by Kuwait, some of their buddies I suppose. They kept setting deadlines for the plane to be refueled, and when the deadline wasn't met, they'd kill a hostage and throw him out of the plane onto the pavement. I guess they did that twice, but when they didn't get their demands, the hijackers finally had to give up..." (p. 5).

Stoll, E., *Family Life*, June, 1988

It is difficult to measure the total affect that America's progress has on a people such as the Amish who are committed to a primitive technology in the midst of a modern world bent on secularization. However, the Amish are a tenacious people and are intent on maintaining their way of life. For family and closeness to one another is everything to the peaceful Amish. With those ties they have survived in America for well over 200 years. Now, the land offered to them by William Penn is cluttered, costly and offers little accommodation for their way of life. However, they will move to wherever is necessary to preserve the faith and sustain the family. As the *Bible* indicates, "If they stop up your wells, move to new lands." As mentioned previously, many Amish have gone to new lands, mostly South American countries, and more are being enticed to these countries by guarantees of complete religious freedom. It is sobering to realize that some peace-loving Amish people are finding it necessary to migrate from America in search of personal freedom in 1990! Yet, it is a fact of life—it is difficult not to be modern man in America today.